CABINETS & VANITIES
A BUILDER'S HANDBOOK

No. 1982
$19.95

CABINETS & VANITIES
A BUILDER'S HANDBOOK

WILLIAM P. GODLEY

TAB BOOKS Inc.
Blue Ridge Summit, PA 17214

FIRST EDITION

FIRST PRINTING

Copyright © 1985 by TAB BOOKS Inc.

Printed in the United States of America

Library of Congress Cataloging in Publication Data

Godley, William P.
    Cabinets and vanities—a builder's handbook.

    Includes index.
    1. Kitchen cabinets.   2. Built-in furniture.
I. Title.
TT197.G55   1986   684.1′6   85-22256
ISBN 0-8306-0982-2
ISBN 0-8306-1982-8 (pbk.)

Cover photograph courtesy of Armstrong World Industries.

Contents

CABINETS & VANITIES
A BUILDER'S HANDBOOK

Introduction

I 'VE LONG BELIEVED THAT A LOW-COST, NO-FRILLS BOOK FOR do-it-yourselfers who are interested in designing and building their own kitchen cabinets and bathroom vanities was sorely needed. I have watched with interest as scores of similar publications were promoted with great "sizzle" and loads of appealing color photos. Amazingly, none of them addressed the basic problem of providing the average home craftsman with the fundamental knowledge and information required to do the job, whether it was building a cabinet or putting up a bookcase. As a consequence, too many creative people have become discouraged and given up on projects simply because they couldn't find answers to their questions.

If you want to make your own bathroom vanities the way professional cabinetmakers do, then this book is for you. Most other books written for do-it-yourselfers assume too much knowledge on the part of their readers. They omit important steps, illustrate major points with vague and often useless photographs instead of highly detailed diagrams, and, in the end, produce cabinets of poor quality—if indeed the projects are ever finished at all.

In preparing this book, I've interviewed several amateur carpenters in my area, and all have expressed a sincere interest in my approach to building cabinets and other things out of wood. Asked to read a draft of Chapter 1 ("Selecting the Right Tools for Professional Results"), they have responded positively and enthusiastically to my detailed, step-by-step approach.

"IF IT'S WORTH DOING, DO IT RIGHT." That has always been my motto as a home and professional craftsman, and I'd like it to be yours, too. The first lesson you should learn in meeting that commitment is one most do-it-yourselfer books neglect or totally ignore: you must plan and estimate each job properly. If you don't, your confidence as a cabinet maker will never have a chance to develop, much less grow. I will show you how to plan and estimate your project so that you'll know from the start exactly how much time must be spent on it and how much it will cost.

Another prerequisite for creating any worthwhile project is skill. You must have enough of it to accomplish the task, and that's why I've devoted so much time and space in the beginning of my book to the fundamental skills required for successful cabinetmaking. There's a good fringe benefit you'll take away from this skill-improvement section, though, because when you're finished with this project, you'll be ready to take on other, more difficult tasks with full confidence in your abilities. As with my bathroom vanities, you'll be able to design, estimate costs, buy materials, build, and finish projects that will be superior in all respects to any mediocre product you might buy ready-made at two or three times the cost.

Many beginning cabinetmakers have great difficulty with the finishing stages. I've taken great care in this book to explain how much fun you can have finishing your cabinets and vanities while at the same time producing a level of excellence you thought could only be attained by a professional.

And finally, I've tried to show you how simple jigs and fixtures can be made from scraps to reduce costly mistakes and waste. Fixtures are the "extra hands" that all cabinetmakers— beginners as well as experienced craftsmen—should learn to use. Jigs allow you to make repetitive cuts and other operations without error.

These are just a few of the advantages you'll gain from using my tested methods and procedures. You'll also discover that quality and efficiency are not assets held exclusively by the professional cabinetmaker. They are yours to enjoy and strive for as well.

Chapter 1

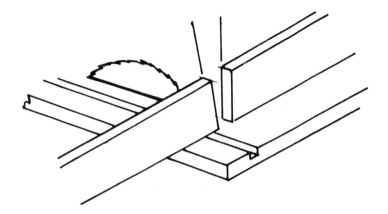

Selecting the Right Tools
for Professional Results

"**T**HE RIGHT TOOL FOR THE RIGHT JOB." IF I'VE HEARD
that axiom once, I've heard it a thousand times. But that
doesn't make it wrong. Unfortunately, some interpret this to mean
that you must rush out before starting a project and buy one of each
tool on sale at the local hardware store. The truth is, you need invest in only a few tools to achieve professional results, but they
must be the right tools.

Remember, our ancestors who built this land did so without
even the simplest power tools. They made fine cabinetry and furniture with their hands and what relatively crude implements were
available at the time, shaping and fastening wood together with
ingenious methods. Some will say these early craftsmen acted out
of sheer necessity. After all, they had little choice but to use what
was available to them. I submit that, were they here now, they'd
be do-it-yourselfers too, working with simple efficiency to create
fine products at low cost.

Today, of course, we can buy almost anything we need, including all kinds of cabinets and bathroom vanities, ready-made
and at a moderate cost. Why, then, should we go to the bother of
doing it ourselves? The main reason, I suspect, is much the same
as it was for our forebears: because it satisfies a deep, instinctive
desire to make things of value and distinction with our own hands.

That doesn't mean we must ignore the blessings of modern

1

technology by limiting ourselves to the tools of early American craftsmen. On the contrary, by taking advantage of the marvels wrought by twentieth century technicians, we can produce our own high quality cabinets with a minimum investment of time and money. A job that might've taken our great-great-grandfathers a week to finish can be done today in a matter of hours.

Now that we've allowed ourselves the luxury of using modern tools with a clear conscience, here's a complete list of the things you'll need (and their approximate prices) to complete the projects described in the following pages:

- 8″ (blade diameter) table saw ($150 & up)
- 1/4″ portable drill ($25 & up)
- 3/8″ power bore bit (about $5)
- 24″ level ($9 & up)
- 24″ rafter or framing square ($10 & up)
- 12″ combination square ($6 & up)
- Claw hammer
- Small nailset (about $2)
- Screwdriver (about $3)
- Assorted sandpaper (aluminum oxide)
- 2″ paint brush (about $5)
- 2″ "C" clamps (about $3 each)

The cabinet shown on the cover of this book could easily be built from start to finish with the tools listed. A power sander instead of sandpapering by hand would speed things up. I discovered long ago that a power sander compensated for my habitual impatience in getting the job done. I have an unfortunate tendency to push on to the finishing stage of any project before the work is really ready for it. Each do-it-yourselfer must recognize his own shortcomings and compensate for them somehow. Actually, unless you're accustomed to using a power sander, you'd be well advised to start out doing the sanding by hand anyway.

WHAT TO LOOK FOR IN A POWER TOOL

Let's assume that you already own a hammer, screwdriver, and the other items listed above except for the power tools. First, a word of caution: although many power tools can perform a variety of tasks, most will only perform their basic functions well. As an example, you can purchase molding heads and cutters for your table saw, and they will do a fair job, depending on your expertise. But for only a few dollars more, you could buy a router that will do the same molding jobs much better and more efficiently. A router will also make fine dovetail joints, in case you decide to build drawers later on. My point is: don't expect any tool to do more than that for which it was designed. By operating on that assumption, you won't be disappointed with mediocre results using special attachments and other subpar accessories.

Of all the power tools in your home workshop, the table saw ranks head and shoulders above the rest. If you don't already own one, it can represent the single most important acquisition of your career as a craftsman. Actually, I can't imagine building a fine cabinet or vanity without a good table saw. It stands to reason, then, that you should buy the very best model you can possibly afford.

A note here about blade size is in order. Why recommend an 8″ saw? Why not buy a 10″ model? After all, isn't it true that bigger is better? It is only when most of the work to be cut involves lumber that is thicker than 2″. It's been my experience that most cabinets can be made with an 8″ table saw. Besides, 8″ blades cost less to buy and sharpen as well. As for blade sizes smaller than 8″, they are usually designed for small hobby work (such as models) and are not suitable for our purposes.

More important than blade diameter is the horsepower of the motor driving the saw. Anything less than 3/4-horsepower simply won't do the job. Be wary of manufacturers' statements that their motors are "comparable to 3/4 (or more) horsepower." Each motor should have a name plate which clearly specifies its advertised horsepower. When buying a new saw, it's possible to purchase one with a greater horsepower motor at a modest increase in cost. I recommend that you give serious consideration to spending a little more for the 3/4-horsepower motor.

Here are a few features you should look for in a new (or used) model:

- Ruggedness.
- Sealed ball bearings: excessive wear in the moving parts of any power tool is the principal cause of failure and loss of precision control.
- Cast metal construction in the table mainframe.
- Smoothly machined work surfaces.
- Easily accessible controls (Fig. 1-1).
- Ability to adjust alignment of table, saw, and other key elements properly.

It is especially important when buying used power tools to check for possible damage to castings and controls. Rarely will a good used tool require new bearings, but whatever you do, don't buy one that has *sleeve bearings*. They are prone to early failure and lack of precision. When you check the classified ads for used power tools, you might notice that certain brands are always available, others aren't. Why? Well, one reason may be that they

are being sold because they did not live up to expectations.

Fig. 1-1. This table saw has large and easily accessible controls.

How much difference does quality make in a power tool? My 8″ table saw (Fig. 1-2) made by Delta (now Rockwell) was a Christmas present way back in 1936! It has never needed repair, never required new bearings, and I can still find spare parts for it if they are needed. More important, it runs today as well as the day I got it. You can't ask for more than that from any tool you'll ever own, I guarantee it. I must confess that several years ago I bought a 10″ Rockwell Unisaw ($1400), because the work I was doing required commercial capacities.

Don't be afraid to ask questions when shopping for a new table saw. Beware of models made of sheet metal or plastic, and make sure that the one you buy can make all the adjustments you'll need. Try not to settle for anything less than the best that you can possibly afford.

One good place to find high quality power equipment is a store that stocks industrial tools. They will carry such top lines as Milwaukee, Rockwell, Porter Cable, Stanley, and Skil. Look for a saw with a solid top made of cast iron, aluminum, or steel (sheet metal extensions on the sides of cast tables are also acceptable).

4

Fig. 1-2. My 8″ tilting table saw.

There should be plenty of room in front of the blade. This will allow you to cut wide boards easily. The *miter gauge slot* should measure 3/4" wide and 3/8" deep. Don't buy a saw with anything different. The miter gauge should also include adjustable "stops" at both sides for making 45° and 90° cuts.

SETTING UP YOUR TABLE SAW

Once your saw has been delivered, setting it up becomes all-important. In fact, how you do this can have the greatest single effect on its future handling and operation. If the saw is new, it should include detailed instructions for assembly and alignment. If so, skip down to the paragraph on *testing alignment*. If you purchased a used machine, I recommend that you write the manufacturer and ask for alignment instructions and a parts list. If possible, include the model number and serial number of your machine; otherwise, describe the saw as best you can.

Whether your saw is old or new, proper alignment is very important. You must set the blade parallel to the miter gauge slot in the table. Do not continue without making this adjustment. Look under the table and locate the mounting bolts (Fig. 1-3) that hold the table to the arbor assembly. They should be oversized bolt heads with washers under them and slots in the casting. Do you also see some small jack screws pushing against metal pads? If you do, you're in luck—your alignment job will be much easier. Loosen the mounting bolts slightly, enough so that when you tap the edge of the table (Fig. 1-4) with a block of wood and hammer it will just barely move. Now, with the miter gauge positioned in the table slot, clamp a stick to the face of the miter gauge so that it protrudes over and just touches a tooth at the front of the blade (Fig. 1-3). The blade should be fully exposed. Then, without unclamping the stick, move the miter gauge to the rear until the stick is located behind the blade (hand-rotate the blade so the tooth used in the beginning is the same tooth at the rear). If the stick just touches the tooth, both front and back, the table is properly aligned (Fig. 1-3). Tighten the loosened bolts and recheck to ensure that no move-

Fig. 1-3. Under table mounting bolts and miter gauge "sticks."

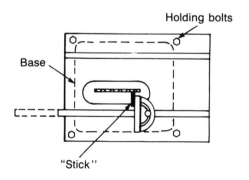

Holding bolts

Base

"Stick"

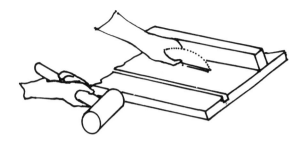

Fig. 1-4. Tap edge of table with wood block to align saw.

ment has occurred. This meticulous operation may seem overly fussy, but it is essential.

Should you discover excessive play between the miter gauge bar and the table slot, inaccuracies can result. Fortunately, this condition can be easily corrected. Simply disassemble the miter gauge from its bar and place the bar on a sturdy vice or solid metal object, and peen the top edges slightly with a ball peen hammer (Fig. 1-5). Keep replacing the bar in the slot until it fits properly.

The *ripping fence* can readily be aligned by loosening the bolts at the front. Move the fence so that its edge is alongside the right miter gauge slot. When the rip fence is exactly even with the edge of the miter gauge slot at both ends, tighten the alignment bolts (Fig. 1-6).

HOW TO CHECK THE ALIGNMENTS

To make sure you've adjusted your saw properly, place a piece of scrap wood with parallel edges on the saw table against the miter gauge and cut it in two. Turn one piece over, with the end you just cut still touching its matching piece (right side up). If, when the pieces are placed against the miter gauge (or a rule) there is only a straight line visible, the adjustment is correct. If, however, there's a V-shaped space, more adjustments are needed (Fig. 1-7). What you have done, by turning one piece over, is to *double the error*, thus making it easier to see. You can now adjust the miter gauge so that it will cut a precise 90° angle. To adjust the saw for 45°, set the miter gauge at that angle and cut another piece of scrap. Place both pieces so the cut side is flush against the miter gauge

Fig. 1-5. Peening miter gauge bar to tighten fit.

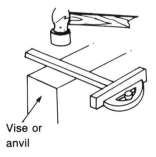

Vise or anvil

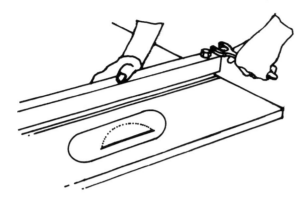

face (Fig. 1-8). If the space between the edges is equal, the cut is an accurate 45°.

To check for proper alignment of table and blade, make sure the blade is fully extended. Again, using some scrap stock with parallel edges—and whose width is about 1/16″ narrower than the height of the blade—make a cut. This time, however, the board should have its edge on the table and its flat side against the miter gauge (Fig. 1-9). After cutting, turn one board over so the top edge becomes the bottom edge. By placing the same ends together, the error—if there is one—will be apparent. On critical work, do not assume that the stop on the saw will give a precise 90° angle between the table and the blade. Always perform this simple test first. If you are uncertain about the cause of your alignment problem, refer to Fig. 1-10.

Once your table saw is ready to operate, don't make the mistake of cutting with dull or improper blades. If you ever sense a "pulling" action, in which the board tends to cut crooked, stop at once. You are either using a dull blade or you are cutting a board that is under extreme stress (for more information on wood stresses, see Chapter 3). Most new table saws come equipped with a combination blade for all-purpose cutting, but you will need other blades for special purposes.

It's important, therefore, that you use the right blade for the job at hand (Fig. 1-11). The most common blade types are: *rip* for fast rough sawing with the grain; *combination* for all-purpose sawing (ripping and cross cutting); *hollow ground combination* for all-purpose finish cutting; *plytooth* for use only on plywood; and *carbide tooth combination* (40 teeth or more) for durability and extremely smooth cuts in most materials, including Formica. This last type is most widely recommended, but it's also the most expensive.

Fig. 1-6. Tighten rip gauge fence adjustment bolts.

Fig. 1-7. Check 90° cut straightness with scrap.

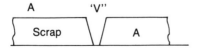

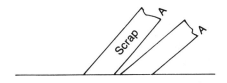

Fig. 1-8. Check 45° of miter gauge.

Always have spare blades on hand, and make sure they are kept clean and sharpened (by a professional, if possible).

SELECTING THE RIGHT PORTABLE DRILL

The nice part about buying a portable drill is that very good models are available at low discount prices. So if you must scrimp, do it here and not with the table saw. You can buy drills with reverse, single, and variable speeds. With a 1/4" drill, variable speed is useful, but reverse isn't. If you can afford two drills, I'd strongly recommend buying a 3/8" drill as well. It can be used to drill metal, to drill large holes in heavy wood, and to install or remove screws. Make sure it has a reversing switch, however.

A word about drill bits is in order, too. There are three common types (Fig. 1-12): *twist* drills, used most frequently for metal; *spade bits* (or power bits), used for drilling fast, rough holes in wood; and *power bore bits*, which feature brad points with round heads and are used for drilling clean accurate holes in wood.

THE POWER SANDER

Among the other portable power tools available, the most useful is probably the sander. One type features a *vibrating* or *orbital* pad, which oscillates back and forth or in a circular motion (Fig. 1-13). Make sure that any sander you buy of this type uses either a half- or quarter-sheet of standard 8 1/2" × 11" sandpaper. The kind that takes a quarter sheet will cost more, but is lighter and operates at a higher speed. This means you can use it with one hand and also get the job done faster. It can also reach into tighter spots than the larger sander. Since I began using a quarter-sheet "block" sander, I've never had occasion to run my larger one—it just gathers dust on the bench.

Fig. 1-9. Check 90° of table and blade.

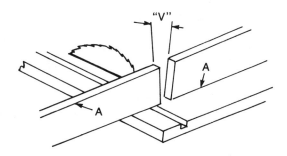

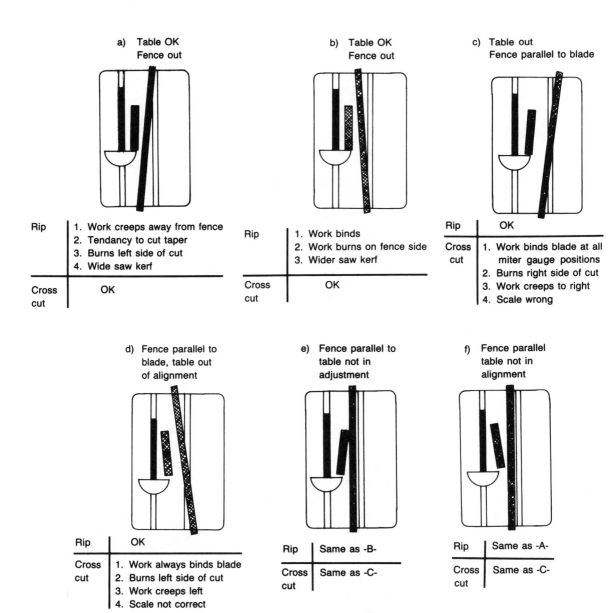

**a) Table OK
Fence out**

Rip	1. Work creeps away from fence 2. Tendancy to cut taper 3. Burns left side of cut 4. Wide saw kerf
Cross cut	OK

**b) Table OK
Fence out**

Rip	1. Work binds 2. Work burns on fence side 3. Wider saw kerf
Cross cut	OK

**c) Table out
Fence parallel to blade**

Rip	OK
Cross cut	1. Work binds blade at all miter gauge positions 2. Burns right side of cut 3. Work creeps to right 4. Scale wrong

d) Fence parallel to blade, table out of alignment

Rip	OK
Cross cut	1. Work always binds blade 2. Burns left side of cut 3. Work creeps left 4. Scale not correct

e) Fence parallel to table not in adjustment

Rip	Same as -B-
Cross cut	Same as -C-

f) Fence parallel table not in alignment

Rip	Same as -A-
Cross cut	Same as -C-

Fig. 1-10. Alignment problems and cures (above).

The other type of sander is the *belt* model (Fig. 1-14), which uses a continuous belt of sandpaper. I found a moderately expensive belt sander (3"-×-21" belts costing about $90) to be extremely useful. Unless you intend to do more than the average amount of woodworking, though, I'd advise against making this investment. Using a belt sander requires more skill than the pad-type, so if and when you do buy one, practice with it before you tackle that special job, such as making raised panel doors. A belt sander is almost essential for that kind of work.

Fig. 1-11. Various blade types.

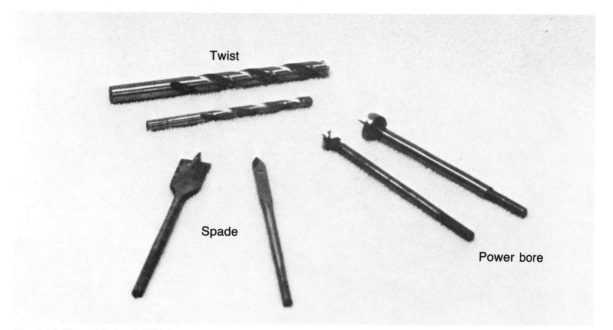

Fig. 1-12. Three kinds of drill bits.

Fig. 1-13. Orbital sanders.

Fig. 1-14. Belt sander.

Sandpaper is a name that covers all kinds of abrasive papers. I strongly recommend using what is called *production* paper, which is coated with particles of aluminum oxide (instead of sand). Dollar for dollar, it's a much better buy and does an excellent job. It also lasts longer. The numbers printed on the back of each sheet indicate the degree of fineness or coarseness, with the largest number representing the finest grade of paper. For hand-sanding and pad-sanding of wood, you need only three grits: 80, 100, and 120. For final finishing of varnished surfaces, 240-grit cabinet paper, followed by wet-or-dry 400-grit, is recommended.

Another handy shop tool for cabinet work is the portable *router* (Fig. 1-15). Unless your plans call for many rounded or molded edges, a router isn't necessary. If you do decide to invest in one, remember that horsepower is less important than speed. A motor that is threaded into the base of the router is much easier to use. I wish someone had once told me what I have just told you: it would have saved a lot of frustration—and cash! When buying tools, always spend plenty of time looking and learning about them first. And the higher the price tag, the more time should be spent on this learning process.

I've found that chain stores carry most power tools at good prices, but often the sales people don't know the first thing about what they're selling. Don't be afraid to "comparison shop." You'll

Fig. 1-15. Router, rack, and pinion.

be amazed at the differences in price for exactly the same tools. Don't be fooled by look-alikes, and compare makes and models carefully. Also, don't overlook mail order sources, such as Silvo Hardware, US Tool, Brookstone, and those who advertise in magazines like *Fine Woodworking*. I've purchased all kinds of tools this way with very good results.

BASIC HAND TOOLS

Thousands of hand tools are available, each one serving its own special purpose. The basic do-it-yourselfer should have most of the following items in his workshop (Fig. 1-16).

- A set of three or more regular screwdrivers
- A set of three or more Phillips screwdrivers
- A set of wood chisels (1/4″, 1/2″, and 1″)
- A 24″ level
- Two or more sets of pipe clamps
- A small jack plane
- A set of dowel gauges

Fig. 1-16. Some basic hand tools needed in cabinetry and woodwork.

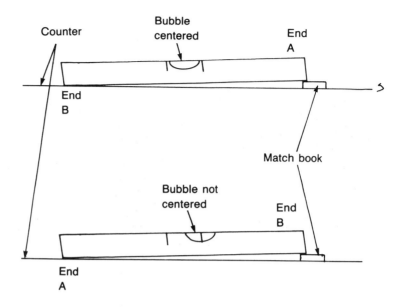

Fig. 1-17. Check level vials and use matchbook to adjust.

Most craftsmen try to get by with no level, or at best a small 6″ one. Unless you're building a doll's house, you should have at least a 24″ level with adjustable bubble vials (if possible). To verify its accuracy (Fig. 1-17), rest the level you intend to buy on a counter edge in the store. If it doesn't show level, put a matchbook cover or something similar under the end furthest from the bubble. Adjust this shim until the bubble is exactly between the lines. Now reverse the level (end for end) leaving the shim where it is, and check the bubble again. Is it still centered between the lines? If not, don't buy it (unless each bubble vial can be individually adjusted).

The other bubbles, usually near the ends, are for plumbing vertical surfaces like walls. To check these for accuracy, find a vertical surface and repeat the process outlined above. Some vials are adjustable, which enables you to make adjustments so that your level will read perfectly every time. Obviously, a level that doesn't read properly isn't worth much.

Combination squares and *framing squares* should be checked for accuracy prior to purchase. The sad fact is, precision tools are sometimes not very precise. If your squares don't always indicate 90°, you'll have one heck of a time trying to build quality cabinets! Here's how to make an accurate check: place the square along a flat surface and draw a light pencil line along its edge (Fig. 1-18). Then, with the square resting on the same plane, turn it over and draw a second line on top of the first. If the two lines coincide or are parallel, the square is true.

Whatever tools you buy, avoid buying them "on sale" unless you are sure of their quality and know the reputation of the

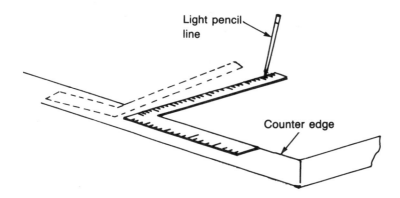

Light pencil line

Counter edge

Fig. 1-18. Check framing square for accuracy.

manufacturer. Many impulse buyers head for the hardware store bargain counters, which are usually marked, "any tool for 99 cents." Forget it! These tools are invariably worthless, unless they are used as "throw-away" tools. Nearly everyone owns a screwdriver that has been used as a chisel, pry bar, scraper, or even a paint mixer. That's ok so long as you relegate it to that all-purpose role. But don't use a good screwdriver for any purpose other than the one for which it's meant; otherwise, you could end up defacing a beautiful piece of cabinetry or injuring yourself because the tool slipped.

CLEANING

Whether your tools are made of steel or aluminum, it's important to keep them clean. With steel tools, wipe them with a clean rag to which a few drops of oil (SAE 10-30 or the like will do) have been added following each day's work. Tables on power tools, because they are machined, are very prone to rust. They, too, may be wiped clean with a rag and a few drops of oil added to it.

This practice, while great for keeping rust off the surface, leaves more oil than desired, so don't be careless about the amount of oil applied. Use too much and the excess may land on the unfinished wood surface; use too little and rust will appear. One solution is to apply a quality car wax, such as Simonize, on the flat machined surfaces once or twice a year. Make sure you first remove any grease or oil from these surfaces with mineral spirits. The metal will remain rust-free, and your work will stay clean and move freely across most metal surfaces. In addition, gum and pitch can be removed from all circular saw blades with a rag and some lacquer thinner.

SHARPENING

There's an old saying: "Nothing succeeds like success." When it comes to sharpening tools, that truism is right on the mark. Down through the years I've learned many ways to sharpen tools and no doubt there are many more I haven't heard about. I've bought sharpening aids and fixtures that turned out to be complete wastes of time and money; I know other craftsmen who bought the same things and found them nothing less than godsends. So even here, how one sharpens his tools can be a matter of personal preference.

Proper sharpening of your tools, no matter what method you use, is as important as proper selection. Strange as it may seem, knowing when your tools are dull is equally important. "When they no longer cut," is not the right answer, for when tools have reached that point, they have long since passed the right time for sharpening. One way to tell is with a strong magnifying glass or jeweler's loupe. Compare the magnified sharp teeth on a new blade with one that has been used (Fig. 1-19). Note that the teeth on the used blade don't have the sharp corners you've observed on the new one. If in doubt, it is always wise to switch to a new blade or saw; if there's an improvement, your old one needs sharpening. If you ask, "Why not just keep using the new blade?" My answer is, "Because you should always have replacements on hand."

Using a dull tool generates heat, which can increase to a point where the temper is drawn out of the cutting edge. When this happens, resharpening will only give your tool a temporary edge; it will become dull again almost as soon as you use it.

Vital Signs of Dullness

On Circular Saws:

- Change of wood color on either side of cut.
- Wood "walks" or pulls to one side.
- Blade has "varnish" just below teeth.
- More effort required to push work through saw.

On Hand Saw Blades:

- Has to be forced through work.

Fig. 1-19. This close-up shows sharp versus dull teeth.

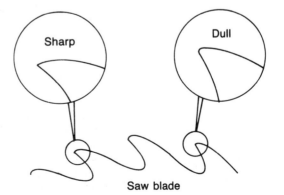

Saw blade

- Sawdust very fine.
- Varnish on blade.

On Chisels and Planes:

- Light can be seen on cutting edge.
- Nicks and notches can be seen.
- Too much effort to move plane.
- Plane shavings are not smooth and clean.

Fig. 1-20. Cup stone used for sharpening.

• Hammer required to use chisels.

The simplest solution, of course, is to have dull blades sharpened by a professional. You'll find them listed in the Yellow Pages. But if you elect to sharpen your own tools, here are a few basic rules to follow. They can help ensure keen edges on everything from chisels and plane blades to shaper cutters and planer knives.

• Planer knives are usually ground to 30° and wood chisels to 35°.
• I once mounted a *cup stone* (Fig. 1-20) on a 1/4" arbor and chucked it in my drill press. It proved an excellent sharpener for grinding chisels and plane blades. With it, I can control the grinding speed as well as the depth of cut.
• Extreme care should be taken to ensure light cuts (.001 = paper thickness); excessive ones will overheat the tool and destroy its temper.

Chapter 2

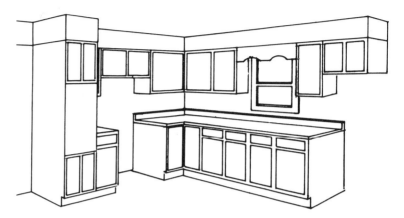

Designing and
Measuring Your Cabinets

N OW THAT YOU'VE ACQUIRED ALL THOSE NICE NEW TOOLS or have rejuvenated your old ones, you're ready to begin work on that new cabinet. Let me offer you a word of caution: if you cannot at this point resist the urge to build something, then try making a bird house or whatever else it takes to avoid jeopardizing your major project. Patience is definitely a virtue in this instance.

Before you pick up one stick of wood, you must carefully plan and design your cabinets—a process that can, believe it or not, take as long as it does to build them. Still, it's far less costly to make mistakes on paper than in the shop.

With your project carefully planned out on paper, you can actually create an accurate image of the finished cabinet. Figures 2-1 and 2-2 are sketches of a typical bath and kitchen. You'll know what it will look like, how it fits in the room, its proportions, style, and color. Good design allows you to satisfy all your needs while at the same time making optimum use of your materials. For example, making a cabinet an inch or two larger can sometimes prove more functional without costing more; it simply "wastes" less. Conversely, reducing the dimensions slightly may also lower the cost significantly. The point is, whatever time you spend designing the cabinet will result in decisions that best suit you. This same process will provide you with sketches and a materials list, which can help you obtain the best competitive prices from a variety of

21

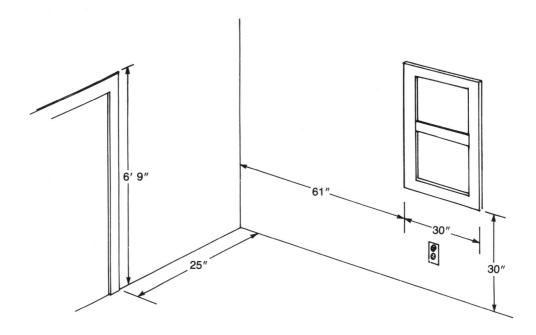

Fig. 2-1. Sketch of bathroom showing dimensions.

sources. Your shopping expedition may also turn up sources and materials you might not have considered before, such as a rarely visited lumberyard where enough good boards of butternut are available to complete your project. Don't be bashful about bargaining for such scraps. The lumberyard may not have the exact length of boards you need, but if you can buy them at a good discount, it may be worth taking what they have. The important thing is to make sure you have enough wood to do the job.

HOW TO MEASURE FOR YOUR CABINETS

The first step is to make a sketch of your kitchen or bathroom as you would like it to look when finished. You don't have to be a professional designer or artist to do this. A very rough picture, similar to Fig. 2-2, is more than adequate.

The kitchen, because it serves so many important functions and requires more cabinetry, is by far the most difficult and costly room in the house to design. Consider for a moment the purpose of the kitchen: it is really the hub in the home around which life revolves, is it not? After all, a significant portion of a family's budget is spent on food and items that end up in this room. Therefore, it would be wise when planning your new cabinets to study the traffic pattern in your kitchen along with its other functions. For example, the kitchen is commonly used for food storage, food preparation, cooking, entertaining, dining, and perhaps laundry as well. Are the new cabinets meant to store food? If so, make allowances for bulky

Fig. 2-2. Sketch of kitchen with pro-
jected cabinet heights.

things like cereal boxes. Will new appliances be bought as part of
the remodeling? If so, figure in their dimensions carefully. You don't
want to build a beautiful cabinet only to find the appliances won't fit!

Designing vanities for the bathroom is not nearly so difficult.
Whether you are doing over an old bathroom or building a new one,
existing or planned plumbing fixtures will dictate the location of
the vanity. Also, make sure the new cabinet doesn't cover an elec-
trical outlet. The rough sketch in Fig. 2-1 illustrates more than ade-
quately what's needed. Such a plan or design can create an image
of exactly what your cabinet will look like, how it fits in the room,
its proportions, style, and even color. Designing allows you to op-
timize the interface between your needs and the most efficient use
of materials.

Obviously, before any drawings and materials lists can be made,
you will need to know the dimensions of the space that is being
allocated for your cabinet. Let's assume that you're building a bathroom vanity cabinet. (The process I'm about to describe, by the
way, can be applied to building any cabinet or piece of furniture.)
Let's assume also that your new bathroom has a door on a side wall
and a window on the same wall where the cabinet will be placed
(Fig. 2-1). Having decided that the vanity will be 34″ high (an
average height in most homes), make several light marks on the
wall where you've decided the cabinet should go—in this case, the
corner. A corner placement can also help demonstrate how to compensate for out-of-square and out-of-plumb conditions.

First, measure from the corner to the point where the right top
side of the vanity will abut ("A" in Fig. 2-3), and make a light mark.
Repeat this measurement near the floor, then use a level to determine whether the marks are plumb. They probably won't be, so

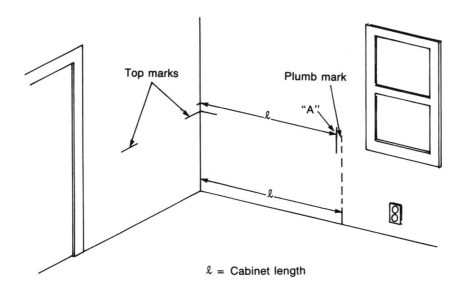

ℓ = Cabinet length

some adjustments may be necessary. Either the top or bottom mark will have to be moved until the right side of the cabinet is plumb. Make a new mark there, and then measure how far you had to move the original mark. Let's call this distance "X," which represents the minimum overhang required on the left side of the cabinet face ("B"). This will compensate for the out-of-plumb situation created on the end wall.

Is the angle between the two walls out of square? Is so, further adjustments are needed (Fig. 2-4). Place the short leg of a framing square flat against the back wall and along the floor, then slide it

Fig. 2-3. Determining plumb dimensions.

Fig. 2-4. Checking squareness of angles between walls.

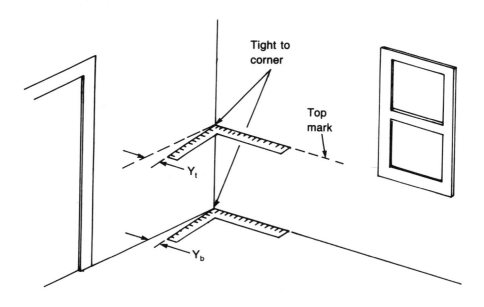

against the end wall to check its squareness. If the back of the square hits the wall first, measure the distance from the long leg of the square to the end wall. Let's call this measurement "Y_b." Repeat the same procedure at the point where the cabinet top will butt the wall and call that distance "Y_t." In a "worse case" scenario, the wall-floor angle (Y_b) and top wall-to-wall angle (Y_t) will both exceed 90°. In that case select the larger of Y_t or Y_b and add it to "X" (the out-of-plumb distance measured above).

The next step is to locate the *studs*, which are the vertical structural members of the wall. Studs are usually 16″ on center, with roughly 14 1/4″ of space between them. So if you can find one, it's usually easy to locate the rest. Studs can be located with a stud finder or simply by tapping the wall and listening for a "hollow" or "solid" sound. When you find a solid area, drive a small finishing nail into the wall to make sure it hits a stud. Once all the studs have been located (Fig. 2-5), your final sketch or drawing should include all the information needed to design the kind of cabinet you want in the space allotted.

SKETCHES AND WORKING DRAWINGS

In designing the cabinet itself, some decisions must now be made. First, study Fig. 2-6 carefully; it shows casework nomenclature to

Fig. 2-5. Mark stud location on walls.

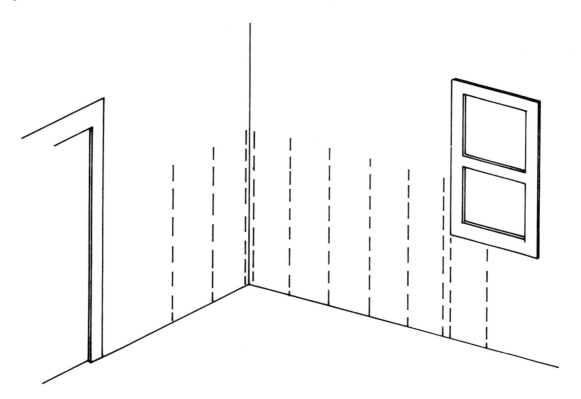

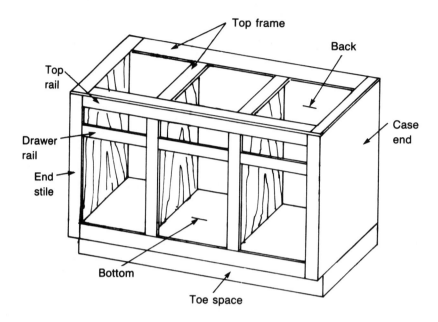

Top frame

Back

Top rail

Case end

Drawer rail

End stile

Bottom

Toe space

Fig. 2-6. Sketch of vanity with nomenclature.

which we will refer later on. Having already decided how wide the cabinet will be, and how deep (most vanities measure 22"), you must ask yourself: will it require one door? Two? More than two? Doors can be as narrow as 5" or 6" or as wide as 24". I wouldn't recommend either extreme, for in my experience extra wide or narrow doors prove too awkward for most practical purposes.

The vertical members of a cabinet door are called *stiles*, while the horizontal ones are *rails* (Fig. 2-7). If, for example, your vanity will measure 48" wide, and the stiles for the cabinet face frame are 2" wide (Fig. 2-8), then you should plan to make three doors covering 40" of open space each (48" less 8"). Divide 40 by 3 (number of doors), and your holes should equal 13 1/3" in width. Because we cannot measure that fraction readily with a common rule or tape, we will accept a dimension for the face frame of 13 5/16" per door opening (Fig. 2-8). Most doors include "lips" that are 3/8" wide, but because we do not want the doors to bind—and space is needed for the hinges—we now add 1/4" per side for the lips. That makes the overall door width 13 13/16" (13 5/16" + 4/16" + 4/16").

The door height is calculated in the same manner. Assuming the doors are flat-paneled, the frames should be 1 3/4" on all sides. If the doors are to be wider than the above, then you may want to make the door rails and stiles wider too; but if the doors are narrower, I'd advise against making the stiles and rails narrower. There won't be enough room for mounting hinges, knobs, or *tenons* (which fasten the rails and stiles together).

As you can see, it's extremely important to have good

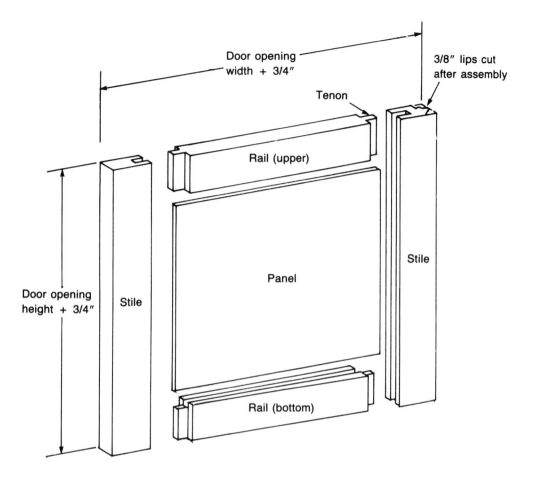

Fig. 2-7. Sketch of door assembly.

sketches of your cabinet and all its parts on hand. Before we go any further, let's make an overall sketch of the *casework*—that's the cabinet without doors, drawers, or face. Most cabinet cases are made from plywood. I usually make mine with 1/2" birch veneer plywood. Your casework sketch or drawing should look something like Fig. 2-8. Next, you'll need a drawing of the *face piece*—the frame that fastens to the front of the case and delineates the openings for drawers and doors (Fig. 2-9). Face pieces can be joined together with *half-laps*, *mortise and tenon*, and *dowels* (Fig. 2-10). I have selected *doweling* because on its relative ease and simplicity. This subject, along with the use of dowel gauges, is discussed in Chapter 4.

Note in Fig. 2-8 that the end stiles—the vertical pieces—are the same height as the face, while the inner stiles are measured to fit between the upper and lower rails. This allows for trimming the face upon installation of the cabinet without having to deal with the end grain of the upper and lower rails—the horizontal pieces.

Wall cabinets are nearly universally 12" deep and 30" high.

In the figure, the following labels appear: Door opening width + 3/4", 3/8" lips cut after assembly, Tenon, Rail (upper), Stile, Panel, Stile, Door opening height + 3/4", Rail (bottom).

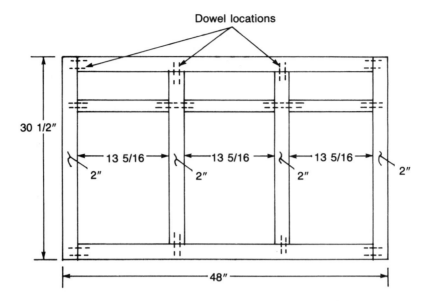

Dowel locations

30 1/2"

13 5/16   13 5/16   13 5/16

2"   2"   2"   2"

48"

You can make them any depth or height you'd like. The widths, or course, are a function of kitchen design. Commercial cabinets come in widths starting at 12" and increasing to 48". The casework for a wall cabinet is identical to the base cabinet except for three things: the shallower depth; a top is used to replace the top frame (the top, in this case will be the same as the bottom); and there are 1"-×-3" support pieces for mounting to the wall. Most fre-

Fig. 2-8. Cabinet face piece dimensions.

Fig. 2-9. Face piece labels.

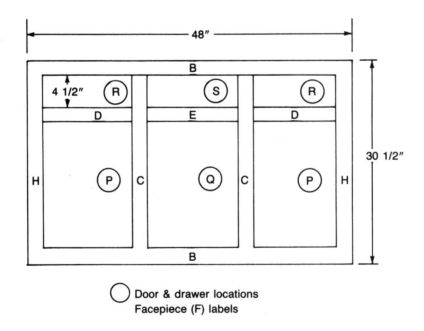

48"

B

4 1/2"   R   S   R

D   E   D

H   P   C   Q   C   P   H   30 1/2"

B

◯ Door & drawer locations
Facepiece (F) labels

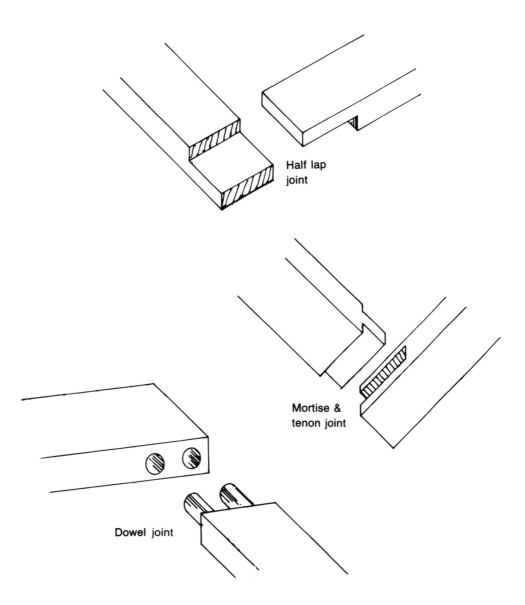

Fig. 2-10. Half-lap, mortise and tenon, and dowel joints.

quently, the shelves in wall cabinets are adjustable and are held up with dowels or shelf supports available commercially. I have, when the situation dictated, made wall cabinets 20″ deep to match a wall oven. That way the 12″ wide cabinet between the oven and refrigerator didn't seem so hidden and inaccessible. Typical cabinet dimensions are shown in Fig. 2-11.

MATERIALS LISTS

So that the materials lists can be referenced back to the drawings,

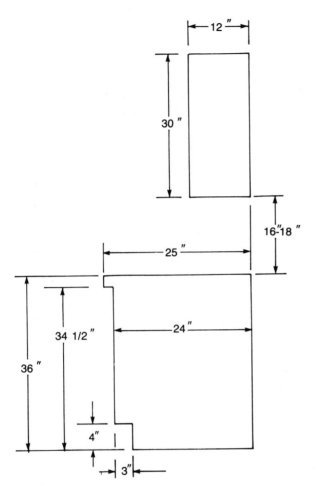

all parts should be labeled in some fashion. I simply use the alphabet, but you can use your own system. For purposes of clarity, I omitted these labels in the original drawings; so now these drawings are repeated here with their labels (Figs. 2-12 and 2-13). Note that whenever a piece is the same size as another, I have given it the same label.

Fig. 2-11. Typical cabinet dimensions.

Table 2-1. Casework Materials List.

Label	Qty	Description	Size
CA	2	end panel	1/2 × 34 × 20
CB	2	divider panel	1/2 × 27-3/4 × 19-3/4
CC	1	bottom	1/2 × 46-1/2 × 19-3/4
CD	2	top frame	3/4 × 3-1/2 × 46-1/2
CE	4	top frame sides	3/4 × 3-1/2 × 19-3/4
CF	12	top frame gusset	1/4 × 4 × 4
CG	1	back	1/4 × 33 × 47

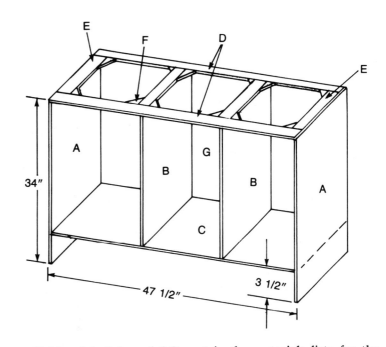

Fig. 2-12. Casework labels.

Tables 2-1, 2-2, and 2-3 contain the materials lists for the various portions of the cabinet. Note that CB, CC, and CE are 1/4″ narrower than the end panels (CA). That's so the back of the cabinet can be recessed, thereby avoiding exposure on the sides. If neither end of the cabinet will show, this reduction in width is unnecessary; the back can simply be installed over the dividers and sides (remember, though, to increase its dimension accordingly).

Fig. 2-13. Door labels.

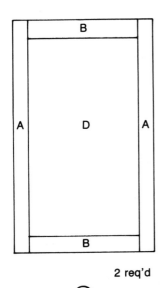

2 req'd

P

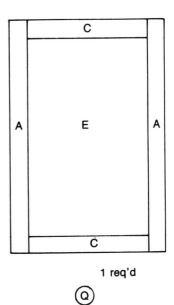

1 req'd

Q

Label	Qty	Description	Size
FA	2	face end stile	3/4 × 2 × 30-1/2
FB	2	top & bottom rails	3/4 × 1-3/4 × 44-1/2
FC	2	divider stiles	3/4 × 2 × 27
FD	2	drawer rails	3/4 × 1-3/4 × 13
FE	1	center drawer rail	3/4 × 1-3/4 × 14

Note in Table 2-2 that the length of the face end stiles (FA) allows the top edge of the bottom rail to run flush with the casework bottom (CC). This level surface (between the frame and case) will allow easier cleaning of the space behind the doors.

Although drawers will be covered in Chapter 7, the list in Table 2-3 includes the drawer *face*, which is defined here as a special panel covering the space above the doors.

Table 2-2. Cabinet Face Materials List.

Table 2-3. Doors and Drawers Materials List.

Label	Qty	Description	Size
DA	6	door stiles	3/4 × 2 × 30-3/4
DB	4	(P) door rails	3/4 × 2 × 10-1/2
DC	2	(Q) door rails	3/4 × 2 × 11-1/2
DD	2	(P) panels	1/4 × 10 × 26-1/4
DE	1	(Q) panel	1/4 × 11 × 26-1/4
DF	2	(R) drawer face	3/4 × 5 × 13-1/2
DG	1	(S) drawer face	3/4 × 5 × 14-1/2

Chapter 3

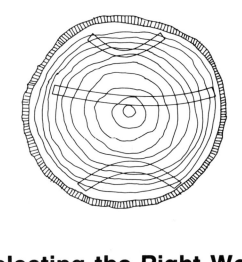

Selecting the Right Wood

HOW MUCH DO YOU REALLY KNOW ABOUT WOOD, THAT marvelous material we all work with? Do you know, for example, that wood is dimensionally unstable and is always moving? Do you know how it reacts after it is cut and dried? What happens to it with the passage of time? Hopefully, the cabinets that result form your labors (and this book) will be kept in use for many years to come. I always like to feel that I'm creating the antiques of tomorrow, and that years from now someone will admire my work enough to acquire it. You, too, should feel that way, because, after all, your work represents your newly learned skills, your personality and creativity.

Most of you are aware that growing trees have rings that represent their annual growth. You may not know, however, that a tree grows from the inside out. To put it another way, the closer to the center of the tree, the older the wood. Thus, the outer wood on a tree is the youngest. The older the wood, the smaller the pores; therefore, the wood near the center contains less moisture. Hence, it will shrink less during the drying process. Conversely, the outer wood has more moisture and will shrink more during the drying process. Cabinets and furniture made from wood with large pores will naturally pick up more moisture during the summer months, thus expanding more than "old wood." Knowing this should help you understand why, when gluing up boards, you should glue younger wood to younger wood; this will help prevent uneven joints due to differences in expansion between old wood and new wood.

Incidentally, by "old wood" I don't mean lumber that was bought ten or more years ago, or that "new wood" was purchased last week. The terms are only used to define from where in the tree the board came. Often the outer wood is called *sapwood* and the inner part *heartwood*. Heartwood is harder, denser, has more color, and usually contains far less knots.

Our forebears created the panel door to allow the wide boards to "move" as they changed dimensions each season. The relatively narrow pieces of wood used to make the stiles and rails (frame) for the panel doors change relatively little with the passing seasons; hence, younger wood can be used.

WOODS: USE, SELECTION, AND COST

Should your cabinet be made of pine, poplar, oak, cherry, or plywood? If this is your first project, perhaps you should choose pine to convey a colonial or early American look. Pine is also the most common species of wood and is readily available in most parts of the country. Many different grades are available, too, ranging from *D-select* to *#3 common*. The cost will vary upward as the number and size of the knots decreases. D-select pine, for example, can cost as much as good hardwood. Hardwoods, by the way, come from deciduous trees (those that lose their leaves each year), while softwoods derive from coniferous trees (those that retain needles year-round). Common native hardwoods vary in "hardness" from poplar to maple, as does their ease of workability.

If you consider knot-free wood essential for your cabinet, a suitable hardwood, such as cherry, should be considered. Number 2 common can, with careful selection, yield portions that are select (knot-free) and sufficient for your needs. The remaining portions of the wood can be used where the knots won't show, although in some cases knots can actually enhance the beauty of a cabinet.

Modern methods of harvesting lumber use what is called *flat sawing*. The tree trunk is placed on a rolling bed or carriage that is driven past the saw blade lengthwise, advancing sidewise after each cut of a desired thickness. In the first boards that are cut, the tree's growth rings appear to lie nearly flat along the board; as the saw nears the center of the tree trunk, these growth rings become almost parallel to the thin edge of the board (or "slab"). These are the boards which, after seasoning and planing, become the choice ones. Boards with the growth rings running straight through them (see Fig. 3-1) are similar to "quarter-sawed" boards. They will tend to *warp* or *cup* and shrink much less than the outer cuts, because the growth rings extend through the board, and because there is a high proportion of "old" wood.

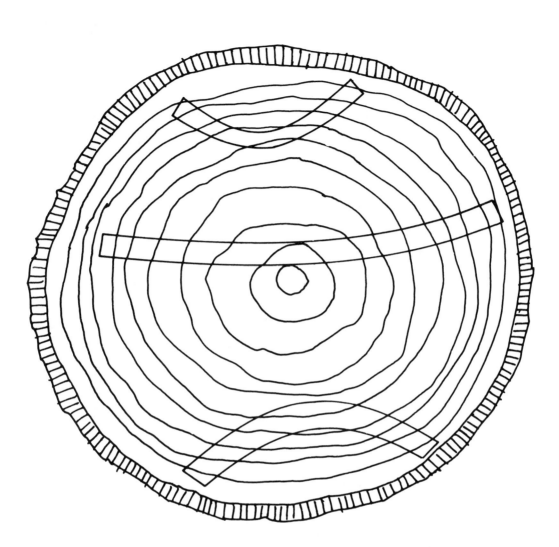

Fig. 3-1. Growth rings can show part of the log from which the board came.

Do not hesitate to ask the salesman or yardman to let you select your own boards. Almost always, he will allow this, particularly if you promise to put the boards back in the same condition as you found them. As a matter of principle, I will not patronize any lumberyard that won't let me select my own boards. I suggest you adopt the same attitude.

As you sort through the lumber pile, bear in mind that what you're looking for are boards that will allow you to cut out the clear or select pieces needed for the rails and stiles on the face and doors. I have found that a measuring tape or rule is a necessity; it allows you to check lengths and widths between the knots before you buy. Don't ignore the boards that have large loose knots in them; I often find that these boards contain large areas of select wood that were probably passed over by previous buyers.

Here's another hint when selecting boards: be flexible. Don't go to the lumberyard in search of a 1-×-6 and look through the 1-×-6s only. Sometimes other board sizes or lengths contain better lumber for your purposes. This may make it necessary to purchase more lumber than you need but the end result will be superior. Furthermore, you'll have some good lumber left over for the next project.

KEEPING COSTS IN LINE

To estimate how much each wood will cost for your project, check the approximate cost ratios listed in Table 3-1 for commonly used wood species. For example, let's assume you've come up with an estimate of $28 to cover the amount of pine needed. Should you now decide that the cabinet would look better in cherry, you'll probably end up spending $53 ($28 × 1.9).

Why not use plywood for the cabinet? I have found that, functionally, plywood is best for casework, where it can be fastened together in a manner that prevents warping and where visible edges don't show or matter. On occasion, I will use birch plywood (lumber core) for door panels. I may also use scraps of 1/2″ plywood (left over from the casework) as drawer dividers. When I do, I glue a

Table 3-1. Comparative Wood Costs.

Wood Species	Cost Ratio	Commentary
Pine	1	Soft, easy to work, glues well for all parts except case work.
Poplar	1	Same as pine; may not be available in some areas; straighter grain.
Oak	1.5	Open grain, hard to work & finish; commonly used for drawer sides.
Birch	1.6	Glues well; can be finished to resemble other woods; medium ease of workability. Most common hardwood used for furniture.
Butternut	1.7	Easy to work, glues well; slightly harder than pine; beautiful finish possible.
Cherry	1.9	Easy to work, glues well; resists splitting better than pine: produces beautiful finishes.
Maple	1.9	Difficult to work due to hardness; beautiful finishes possible. Not recommended for beginner.
Mahogany	2.1	Various grades available; open grain, works same as pine. Softness depends on species.
Walnut	2.8	Same as cherry.

strip of birch along the exposed edges (called *banding*). You'll find that birch plywood costs about as much as solid wood. Although it may be an excellent choice for the casework, it's a poor choice for most other parts of a cabinet.

Chapter 4

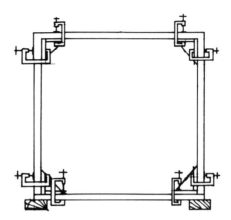

Laying Out and Cutting Materials

BEFORE WE GET INTO THE FINE DETAIL OF THINGS, THIS IS probably a good place to discover how to use a materials list. The materials lists created in the last chapter are breakdowns of all the pieces needed for the various parts of the cabinet. In order to make the purchasing and cutting of the lumber easier, we'll make a new composite materials list showing all the pieces from largest to smallest. With this list, you'll be able to make certain that "available" bargains or "deals" you're able to find in the lumberyard will in fact supply what is needed. Remember, however, you'll want some extra lumber to cover miscuts, damaged, or unusable portions. Table 4-1 is a composite materials list of Tables 2-1 through 2-3.

Those pieces marked with an asterisk are the ones for which special care should be taken in their selection, because they form the front of the cabinet. Rails and stiles for the face and the door panels should be free of knots (unless they are very small and tight). As you physically sort through the lumber pile, keep in mind where the knots are, and whether, as you cut out your pieces, you'll be able to avoid them. Sometimes a few large knots, even loose ones, can be worked around so that you end up with some really select material.

PLYWOOD—1/4 inch			
Size	Qty	Label	Description
33 × 47	1	CG	Back (case)
11 × 26 1/4	1	DE	Panel (door)
10 × 26 1/4	2	DD	Panels (door)
4 × 4	4	CF	Gusset (top)
PLYWOOD—1/2 inch			
19 3/4 × 46 1/2	1	CC	Bottom
19 3/4 × 27 3/4	2	CB	Divider panel
20 × 34	2	CA	End panel
PINE—3/4 (or selected wood)			
* 5 × 14 1/2	1	DG	Drawer face
* 5 × 13 1/2	2	DF	Drawer face
3 1/2 × 46 1/2	2	CD	Top frame
3 1/2 × 19 3/4	2	CE	Top frame
* 2 × 30 1/2	2	FA	End stile (face)
* 2 × 30 3/4	6	DA	Door stiles
* 2 × 27	2	FC	Divider stiles
* 2 × 11 1/2	2	DC	Door rails
* 2 × 10 1/2	4	DB	Door rails
* 1 3/4 × 44 1/2	2	FB	Top & bottom rails

SETTING UP YOUR TOOLS

Table 4-1. Complete Materials List.

Learning how to set up your tools will minimize the number of errors and speed things along. When using the table saw, make sure that you have the appropriate blade in place. Because, in our example, we're building a vanity, we'll be starting out by cutting the 1/2″ plywood for the casework, hence you should have a plytooth blade on the saw. In all probability, you will have a full sheet of plywood to cut. There are two ways to handle something this large and awkward: have an oversize saw table and a "run out" table or roller; or precut the plywood on sawhorses with a portable electric hand saw. Usually I will take the latter route. Be careful in your layout to allow space for the less accurate cut made by the hand power saw. Also, when later making the final cuts on the table saw always make sure a "factory" edge is against the rip fence or miter gauge.

Do your utmost to have your cutting organized so that all the pieces being cut to one dimension can be cut at one set-up. If you don't, two things will happen: you'll take longer, because you're making extra setups, and the pieces cut during different setups will have slightly different dimensions.

As the pieces are cut, mark them lightly in pencil with their label and check them off on the composite materials list. That way, you won't cut extra pieces or miss a piece.

The essential first step of stock preparation is obtaining a true face side and edge. These are the surfaces to which all work and measurements are referred. Therefore, proper preparation of a face side and a related edge are important preparatory steps in cabinetmaking, or any woodworking for that matter. The saying that a house is no better than its foundation applies in cabinetmaking. The face side must be flat in all senses, with no cupping, no crowning, and no twist from end to end. It is necessary to prepare a side that is flat in width, flat in length, and does not twist (or *wind*, in woodworkers' parlance). To do this, it is necessary to have a straightedge as long as the longest piece used and a pair of *winding sticks*. Winding sticks may be perfectly straight sticks of wood (1- x -3) or they may be two rulers. They should be at least 12″ long so that you will be able to see the wind or twist. If a board is flat and does not wind, then that is the face side and should be so marked. In my case, I use an "F." There are many criteria for selecting which side of the board should be the face. Among them are grain matching, exposure, minor defects or knots on one side only, mixture of heartwood and pulpwood on one side and not the other, and so on.

Sometimes the face side will end up inside the cabinet, and sometimes it should be properly outside. For example, the face side of boards or pieces in a drawer should be inside, while the face side of the face frame should be outside. Frequently the face side will be opposite the best looking side, but don't let this bother you. Remember, the face side is the reference side from which measurements are made and from which machining starts. The "F" or face mark denotes the side of a piece that is either naturally flat in width and length and not winding, or one that has been machined to be so. It must be a statement of fact, not intent; if in an initial layout you desire to show intent, use another symbol or mark.

The face edge is produced using the face side, and it also is flat side to side and end to end and has no wind end to end. Further, the face edge is almost 90° to the face side. All subsequent markings will relate to the face side and edge. Usually, the width is marked and cut first. In other words, all points on the face surface must be in the same plane. It is always best to "cut out" and prepare all stock for a given job at the same time. Doing this will almost always save time, material, and effort and minimize the chance of mistakes. On occasions where it has been impossible to follow this rule, it has only been the fact that I have carefully made materials lists and notes and marked each of the pieces made that has prevented disaster. Restarting a job only a day or two after the initial start always means extra time to determine exactly where you left off after the original start. It goes without saying that if some of the pieces are cut at one time and the rest cut at another time, they will not be exactly the same. This means, of course, that slight differences may compound themselves later on.

Selecting Lumber

Selection of lumber for the job is part of the preparation of stock. If you know what has to be achieved with the pieces of wood, then you have a better idea of which ones to select. If the lumberyard will not let you select your lumber, do not shop there. You must decide whether you will cut all the pieces to the approximate final size, or prepare larger pieces from which you will later cut the appropriate number of smaller pieces later. I have found that I am able to make better use of the available stock by cutting all the pieces to the approximate final size, with allowances for creating the true face surface and edge. The disadvantage of doing it my way is that it will take a bit more time. Frequently, I start out with boards that are 12 feet and longer. Handling boards that size—unless you're in a large very well equipped shop—is, at best, difficult. Using my "composite" list (which starts with largest pieces first), I tentatively rough out how the large board will be cut down. I do this in a manner that allows me to "cut out" knots, checks, or other defects.

You must make the assumption, when dealing with the boards you start with, that none of the faces, edges, or ends are true. To make a point, if your composite materials list shows that all the pieces could be cut from a board 10' long and 12" wide, I can categorically state that you won't be able to get all the pieces you'll need. I have found in practice that I need at least 15 percent more material than the materials list shows. Usually, the figure may end up being 20 to 30 percent more, because of the boards I select or because of the available material sizes. It is wise to have extra stock; after all, you may have calculated wrong or find a piece that is unusable, miscut, or mismachined. I try to have extra stock so that it may be used in setting up my machines and making check cuts.

Rough Cuts and Final Cuts

Cutting each piece of wood twice—one rough and one final—at first glance may seem a waste of time, energy, and material. In a way it is, but I have found this procedure very important in achieving optimum precision. All layout work must therefore take into account dimensions that are at least 1/8" wider and 1/4" longer than necessary. If several boards need gluing together to form a panel, then make the total width of the pieces at least 1/4" wider and 1/2" longer to allow for final sizing and truing up of the ends. To repeat, as you cut each piece, mark it lightly with a pencil. Always cut the largest pieces first. Keep checking your materials list; you may not always be able to cut the largest pieces first, but you will be assuring maximum use of the lumber on hand. Keep in mind too, that when these same pieces are glued together later on, you'll want to "match" the grains; that way, they won't look like disparate pieces. When cutting small stock from a large straight board, you may discover that the smaller pieces are no longer square or even, because a chip or particle of sawdust stuck to the edge. That's another reason for making all rough cuts slightly larger. Marking the materials list as each board is cut also helps keep track of all the pieces needed and whether they have in fact been cut. I recommend a marking system similar to that used in a sawmill (see sample below). A dot represents each piece; thus if ten stiles are needed (because five doors are required) there should be ten corresponding dots on the list.

ie: door stiles . . . .

Without marking the list, you're bound to make mistakes and lose valuable time and money.

Oops!

Let's assume that, after you've ripped all the pieces for the cabinet and have changed the ripping fence adjustment, you discover another piece of the same width is needed. Here's a good way to rip that piece without having to remake the fence adjustment. Set the fence so that it's 1" to 2" wider than the replacement board width desired. Set the work piece (board with the width required) against the rip fence; then rip a scrap piece that is wider than the gap between the blade and work piece (with the work piece acting as a rip fence). Place the sized scrap piece against the fence and rip the additional needed piece, this time using the scrap piece as the fence.

SIMPLE JIGS AND FIXTURES

Cabinetmakers learn to use jigs and fixtures. They allow you to make repetitive cuts and other operations without costly errors and duplication of effort.

It has always astounded me how few cabinetmakers use jigs or fixtures. I've often wondered if they thought it was beneath the dignity and skills of a craftsman. Well, I certainly feel that one should use all the available tricks of the trade to make his job easier or improve the quality of the end product. So, hopefully, you will understand how and why the use of jigs and fixtures can be of great help in avoiding repetitive cuts that otherwise must be laid out each time with a ruler or scale and square. If pieces must be exactly the same, they must either be cut at the same saw setup or by using jigs or fixtures.

My definition of a *jig* is: a device that allows one to make repetitive woodworking operations without laying out each piece. A *fixture*, on the other hand, allows one to hold pieces together while

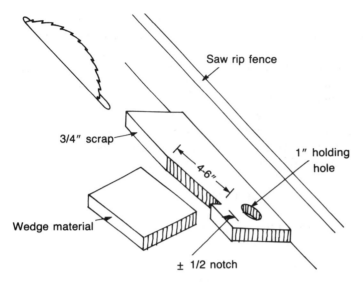

Saw rip fence

3/4" scrap

4-6"

1" holding
hole

Wedge material

± 1/2 notch

working on them (i.e., clamping fixtures that allow you to screw different parts together).

Let's start out with a simple jig used to cut wedges. Why do we want a *wedge jig*? Well, the pieces of your cabinet will not always

Fig. 4-1. Wedge jig can be made from scrap.

Fig. 4-2. Cutting wedges.

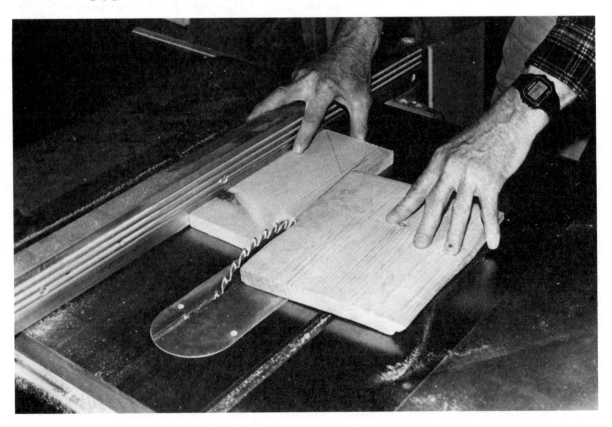

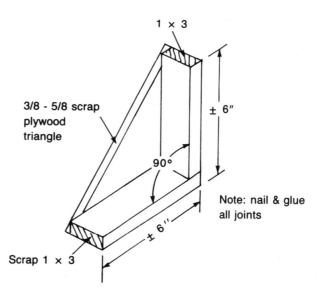

1 × 3

3/8 - 5/8 scrap
plywood
triangle

± 6"

90°

Note: nail & glue
all joints

± 6"

Scrap 1 × 3

Fig. 4-3. Right angle "C" clamp.

Fig. 4-4. Using right angle clamp.

fit perfectly, and I have found that wood wedges made of the same material as the cabinet are invaluable in aligning and fitting the cabinet together. Further, you will probably need quite a few wedges during the process of installing your cabinet, because it is unlikely that the walls and floor will be perfectly straight. Until I started using my wedge jig to make and stock wedges of various woods, I never realized how often they helped me out of a predicament. The jig shown in Fig. 4-1 is very simple to make and certainly should be made of scrap wood. The fact of the matter is, I have several jigs for wedges, some that make long skinny wedges,

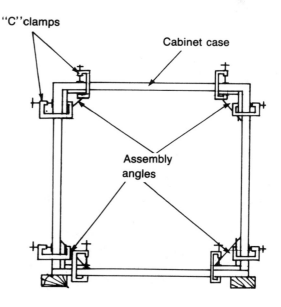

"C" clamps

Cabinet case

Assembly
angles

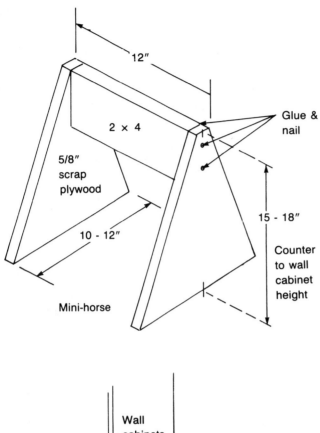

12"

Glue & nail

2 × 4

5/8" scrap plywood

10 - 12"

15 - 18"

Counter to wall cabinet height

Mini-horse

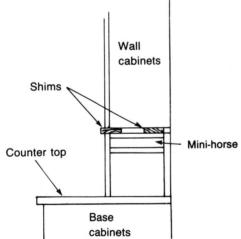

Wall cabinets

Shims

Mini-horse

Counter top

Base cabinets

and one for short thick wedges. Prior to throwing away scrap wood, I get out the wedge jigs and fill up my boxes with wedges made from the scrap (Fig. 4-2).

Another invaluable fixture, the right angle "C" clamp, can also be made from scrap pine and scrap plywood. I used CDX (unsanded plywood sheathing used in construction), but anything will do as long as it's 3/8" or thicker. See Fig. 4-3 for the details of the right-

Fig. 4-5. Making and using a mini-horse.

angle "C" clamp fixture. I have eight of them and constantly use them as extra hands when I am assembling casework. See Fig. 4-4 for details of how this clamp holds the pieces together while gluing and fastening the casework pieces. The larger the cabinet being made, the more helpful the right-angle fixtures are.

Many of my fixtures have evolved out of the frustration of trying to do cabinet construction and installation by myself. The "mini-horse" was created to support the wall cabinets above the countertop while they were being fastened to the wall. A word of caution is in order here. First, of course, it must be used on a counter that has been leveled. Second, the wall cabinet should not rest directly on the "mini-horse," because it will be nearly impossible to remove once the cabinet has been screwed to the wall. Depending on circumstances, I use scraps of 3/4″ pine between the "mini-horse" and the bottom of the wall cabinet. Figure 4-5 shows the details at the "mini-horse."

Perhaps the most useful thing that I created for shop use was my folding "runout" table for the table saw. I suppose the roots of the design for the table derived from my years in building sce-

Fig. 4-6. Folding run-out table.

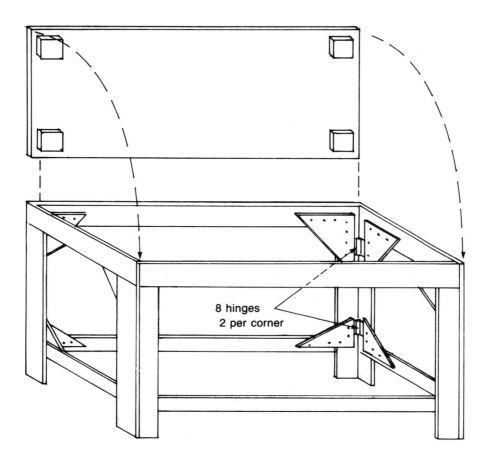

8 hinges
2 per corner

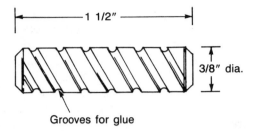

1 1/2"

3/8" dia.

Grooves for glue

nery for amateur theater. To digress for a moment, theater scenery is intended to create an image that appears to be real to an audience. Because space on a stage is limited, much scenery either "flies" up out of the way, or it comes apart and/or folds up. Stage platforms almost always consist of a "top" and a four-sided frame that is hinged at the corners so it will fold "flat." The runout table (Fig. 4-6) is built exactly like a stage platform. The height is very important; it must be about an 1/8″ lower than the height of your saw table. The other dimensions are unimportant. My table is 30″ by 48″ because that was the biggest piece of 1/4″ plywood I had at the time I built it. Why a 1/4″ piece rather than something thicker? I am a firm believer in making things strong but light;

Fig. 4-7. Spiral grooves in dowels can be cut using dowel centers.

Fig. 4-8. Dowel gauges.

perhaps my theater background has something to do with that belief. I use the runout table not only to support long boards being ripped, but also as an assembly table while gluing boards or assembling the casework of a cabinet.

JOINERY

Now that all the pieces have been cut, it's time to decide how to fasten them together. As mentioned in Chapter 2, assembling the face frame and door frames can be accomplished with half-lap joints, mortise and tenon, or doweling (see Fig. 2-10). I have chosen doweling because in many ways it simplifies the cutting of parts to size and their subsequent assembly. Dowels can also be purchased premade. The most common size, and the one we'll use, is 3/8″ diameter and 1 1/2″ long. If you choose to make your own from 3/8″ doweling, you must score or cut spiral grooves prior to cutting to length (as shown in Fig. 4-7).

Dowel gauges are inexpensive and nearly always available in sets of two for each size (1/2″, 3/8″, 5/16″, and 1/4″). You'll probably never require any dowel gauges (Fig. 4-8) other than 3/8″, and you may be able to purchase two of that size alone. When laying out the centers for the dowel holes, be sure to allow enough wood to prevent splitting. Figure 4-9 shows dimensions for drilling for the various pieces used in the vanity. Always drill only the holes on one side of a joint after layout. Drill the holes in the end grain first; it's easier to be precise when drilling the second hole marked by the dowel gauge.

Doweling should be a simple and precise operation—if it's done correctly. Here again, the fact that you've marked each piece will help avoid mix-ups when it comes time to drill for dowels. Once

Fig. 4-9. First hole, dowel dimensions.

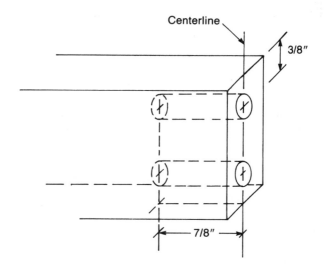

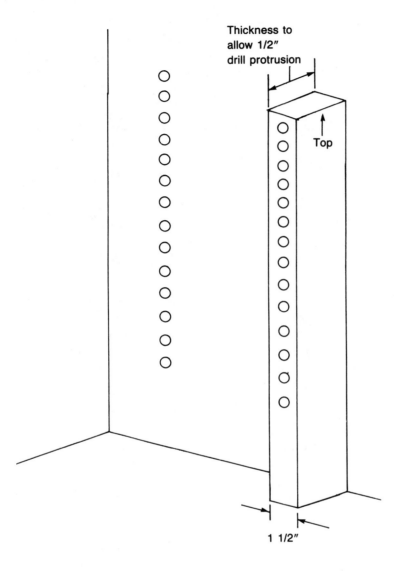

Thickness to
allow 1/2"
drill protrusion

Top

1 1/2"

all holes have been drilled in one side of the joint, place the dowel
gauges in the two holes of one of the joints. Hold the piece con-
taining the dowel gauges firmly on a flat surface (I use the top of
the table saw), then carefully align the mating piece exactly as it
will appear in the final joint. Now tap the piece without holes against
the pins of the dowel gauge. See those small indentations? They
will become the centers for the holes. To make sure the hole is truly
perpendicular, I use a drill press, but there are clever little devices
on the market that enable anyone to make straight holes with a
portable drill. Figure 4-10 shows how to make a drill guide bushing
to allow you to drill the shelf bracket holes so they will be the same
spacing everywhere.

Fig. 4-10. Drill guide for doweling to
support brackets.

Chapter 5

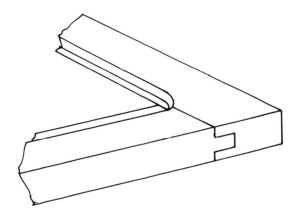

Putting It All Together

ALL WOODWORKERS WANT TO AVOID THE BIG MISTAKES.
Fortunately there are only two things that cause most of
them: undue haste and failure to plan your work progress carefully.
Well planned steps in any woodworking project should include dry-
fitting all pieces together first to ensure that the sizes are correct,
that the pieces are marked correctly, and have all been made or
cut. The best way to minimize this type of error is to double-check
at each step. Dry assembly allows corrective actions such as chang-
ing the width of a piece that was not cut to final size. Discovering
this after you have applied glue means you will have to remove all
the glue from the pieces and make the necessary corrections before
continuing. As I can painfully attest, that's a frustrating and time-
consuming way to go.

Haste, likewise, is an ever present enemy of the woodworker,
whether amateur or professional, and it may well be the major cause
of any lack of consistent quality in your work. Haste can, for example, cause one to cut a board too short, fail to make all the final
cuts, or not cut all the pieces needed. My advice is: slow down.
Enjoy each step of the project and strive for perfection, step by
step. You will be amazed at the difference it makes in the final product (not to mention your disposition).

Do you remember my admonition, "Measure twice, cut once?"
Once you've dry-assembled your cabinet, be sure to measure all

the critical outside dimensions. Do they agree with the ones on your sketch for that allotted space? Do they agree with the ones on your overall cabinet sketch? If they don't, you are probably putting together a cabinet that won't fit where it's supposed to! Do not make the assumption that everything you've done, step by step, is without error. Remember, a mark you made could have been in error, a cut may have been made improperly, or your calculations for part dimensions may have been wrong. So let me modify the "Measure twice, cut once" axiom to: "Measure the assembly dry, then glue once."

GLUES

An adhesive is a material capable of holding two pieces of wood together through surface attachment, and the most common adhesive used in woodworking is glue. Glues are used in a number of ways: to increase the width of boards, to make composites (such as plywood), and to assemble the various parts that go into making cabinets and furniture. Properly speaking, glue is a member of the same adhesive family to which *resins* (such as epoxy), *mastics* (like those used with floor tiles), and *cements* belong.

Natural glues, such as *casein* (a derivative from milk) and hide glues made from the hooves and hides of animals, were once much more popular than they are today. Perhaps the most common family of glues used by today's woodworker is the *polyvinyl resin emulsions.* The common "white" glues, such as Elmer's Glue-All, Sear's white glue, and Evertite by Franklin, are all polyvinyl emulsions. They develop high strength and set rapidly (a clamping time of less than two hours is usually sufficient). They are nonstaining and transparent when dry.

Excessive glue on the surface can clog sandpaper during the subsequent sanding processes. That's because the glue's thermoplastic qualities may cause it to "melt" from the friction. Any glue that gets on the wood surface, therefore, must be removed with a damp cloth or in subsequent finishing; stains will not be absorbed where glue spots remain.

The modified polyvinyl adhesives, which include Elmer's Professional glue, are sometimes called *yellow glue.* They can help alleviate some of the shortcomings of the white glue because of their higher viscosity, which makes them less apt to drip. They also boast better heat and moisture resistance. They will not, however, provide a weatherproof joint the way *urea-formaldehyde* glues can.

Obviously there are many different glues from which to choose, and we have touched on only a few. The right ones to use depend to a great extent on the final application. For cabinet work, where normal temperatures and moistures found in a home are encountered, I have found that the yellow glues do a good job. Unless

I must use another type (because the work will be exposed to the weather, such as on a boat) that's about all I ever use.

The reason that glue sticks two pieces of wood together, contrary to what you may think, is sometimes called *specific adhesion:* namely, a chemical attachment or bond is created by molecular forces between a wood surface and an adhesive. When glue is applied to two surfaces it wets the cell structure of the wood. Pressure is then applied to spread the adhesive uniformly thin and hold things in place until the adhesive solidifies. The best way to apply this pressure is with clamps.

Most glues set to form a glue layer through evaporation. This process allows the molecules to "get together" and form a tight bond. Almost without exception, woodworker's glues will make a stronger joint than the wood being joined. No one wood glue is better than another, but there are variations in tack time, open joint setting time, and closed joint setting time. Some woodworking glues, such as Elmer's Professional, are *freeze stabilized*, while others, such as Elmer's regular white glue, are not.

All woods do not glue equally well. In general, the harder the wood, the more care must be taken to make a good glue joint. Some woods, such as teak, which has natural oils, are difficult to glue and require special procedures to do so satisfactorily. Oak and mahogany may be stained by most glues.

When applying glue, be sure to spread it as evenly as possible. Do not depend on the clamping to distribute the glue, because that will happen only to a point. I have found that when both surfaces are evenly wetted with glue, the results are excellent. I often use a glue brush, which has stiffer bristles than a paint brush. When there's a lot of gluing to be done, I may even use a small paint roller. The only problem with a roller is the messy cleanup job, and the fact that you have to use more glue to wet the roller in the beginning.

If you plan to use glue frequently in your woodworking, consider buying a whole gallon of it. Also, buy one handy applicator bottle of glue and keep refilling it from the gallon container. You'll save a lot of money (it takes about four applicator bottles to equal a quart of glue, and they will cost about the same as the gallon).

I'll admit it's difficult to spread glue evenly. Too little means a *starved joint* and a poor bond. *Double spreading* (a layer on each surface) is the best way to prevent glue starvation. Any "squeeze-out" can be scraped off with a putty knife or simply wiped off with a damp cloth. In tight corners, I've found that a wet toothbrush does a great job cleaning off excess glue.

CLAMPING

The reason for clamping when gluing is to not only keep the pieces together, but to press the glue line so that a continuous, uniformly thin film is created. If all surfaces to be glued were cut or machined to perfection there would be practically no need to press or clamp them together, but such is rarely the case.

It is important that both wood surfaces are in intimate contact with the glue and remain undisturbed until the cure, or *glue set*, occurs. Because there is usually solvent evaporation or loss in the drying process, stresses may develop in the glue line. Using extra glue to fill voids caused by improper dry fitting of the joints prior to gluing will only create excessive stresses and, in all likelihood, weaker joints. The strongest, most effective glue line should be very thin, perhaps only a few thousandths of an inch thick. The amount of clamping pressure varies with the wood density—less is required for pine, for example, and more for hardwoods. Too much pressure, of course, can force too much glue out of the glue line, either through the pores of the wood or simply out of the joint. The less pressure required, the more chances of making a strong joint. The time to make up for poor surface preparation is not during the gluing process.

It's important to remember that after gluing you must allow the joint to reach an equilibrium, because the wood will temporarily swell at the glue line. Immediate finishing of the glue line surface could result in a *dip* (Fig. 5-1) at that point once the wood has returned to its normal moisture content.

GLUING STOCK

When gluing up boards to make wider boards, there are a couple of things to remember. First, always glue new wood to new wood

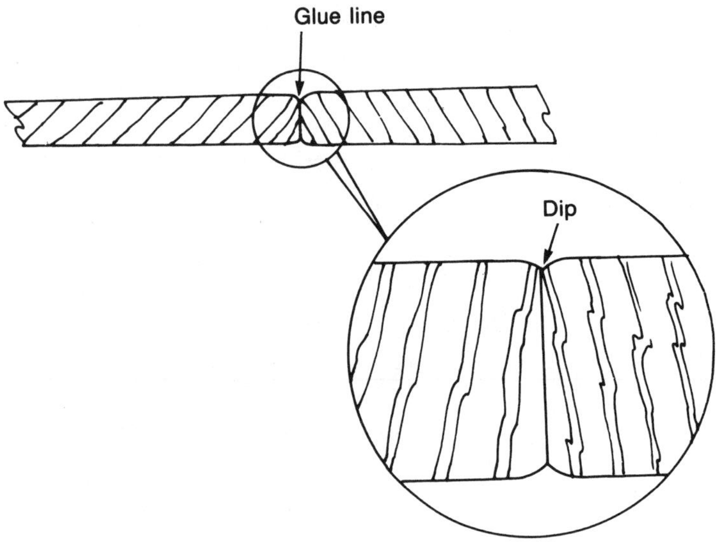

Fig. 5-1. Effects of working too soon after gluing.

Glue line

Dip

Fig. 5-2. Improper gluing of cupped boards.

and old wood to old wood (see Chapter 3). Do not alternate "cupped" boards, because you will be gluing old wood to new wood. What will happen? Well, somewhere down the line an uneven joint or a wavy washboardlike surface will result (Fig. 5-2). I do not recommend the use of dowels when gluing up boards to make wider stock. For one thing, the long grain of the dowel runs perpendicular to the long grain of the boards. Shrinkage will thus differ between the dowel and the board, causing them to move, one with respect to the other. I used to pass boards to be joined through my shaper, because I thought that a glue joint along the edge provided a greater glue surface. I have found, however, that this is not needed, because the joint without such an improvement is still stronger than the wood itself. So why bother?

When you have stock that is to be edge-glued, it is not critical to have a 90° edge on the boards. Both must have been cut with the same blade angle, however, and one of them must be upside down with respect to the other.

The long grain edge of the boards to be glued should be slightly concave (Fig. 5-3). This puts more pressure at the ends of the boards, so that when the glue dries the board will emit moisture at the ends first. The pressure created by the concave edge will then be released. As a result, the ends will be less likely to split or *check*.

There are several reasons for gluing up stock. Perhaps the most obvious reason is to create wider boards than those available at the lumberyard. Another would be to eliminate undesirable defects—for example, a loose knot in the middle of an otherwise select piece. I do not recommend using glued-up stock for a face piece or door stiles and rails. The most frequent usage for gluing boards together is in the creation of door panels. Keep in mind that you should try to match the grain of the two boards so that when they are glued

Fig. 5-3. Gluing slightly concave, long-grain board.

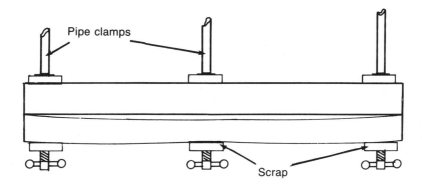

Pipe clamps

Scrap

together the resulting wide board has a grain that looks natural. By laying the boards together and turning the ends one way and then the other, you can easily find the combination that looks best. Also, by selecting and matching the grains properly, the resulting glue line should be invisible to the naked eye. On occasion, when a required panel board was 1/2" narrower than needed, I have glued a 1/4" strip on each side, knowing that when the panel was finished the 1/4" on each edge would be hidden.

In order to keep this first project simple, I have assumed that the door panels are made from 1/4" plywood. That doesn't mean your doors must have plywood panels. In fact several variations of raised panels are possible, including "mock" raised panels made from plywood. Another variation is to glue cane in the opening normally covered by the panel. This is particularly suitable when ventilation is desired. If you decide on a cane panel, the dado on the stiles will have to be modified and splines added. Figure 5-4 shows some examples and variations on doors. If you prefer to have the inner edges of the stiles and rails molded, and you do not want to purchase a router, buy some ready-made molding and glue it in place (Fig. 5-4). If caning is used, rabbeting (routing) for a spline will be necessary (Fig. 5-5).

As you'll recall, the pieces listed in the materials list were all cut oversize because we wanted to cut them to their final size later. We did this because when sawing large boards (whether ripping or cross cutting), it is nearly impossible to achieve precision. The

Fig. 5-4. Variations on door types.

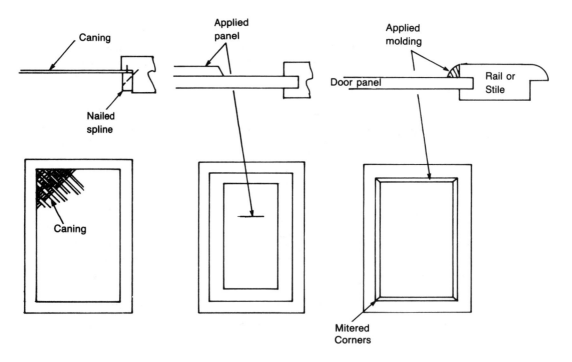

board may be so large that it is awkward to handle, or it may bow or twist after ripping. A tree, as it develops, is subjected to many strains and stresses, such as ice and wind storms. When a limb is blown off, for example, the tree, which is no longer balanced, tends to lean. As the tree continues to grow, it tries to correct this imbalance. Later, after the tree has been timbered and sawn into boards,some of these stresses are relieved. The result may well be several twisted and bowed boards.

FINAL SIZING

Prior to final sizing of the boards, be sure to make one last check of your calculations. Then make all cuts of the same dimensions at one saw setting. In making the final sizing cuts, I can't emphasize enough the importance of using a sharp blade. Why? Because a blade that is not sharp will tend to "walk off" the edge, especially when you're cutting a very thin slice. The result will be sawed boards that are no longer square. Take care, therefore, to check the squareness of each board end after cutting. It's a good idea also to go over all the boards prior to final sizing, marking each reference edge and reference end. Boards without square ends should be cut so that one end is true before proceeding. That may sound like a lot of work, but it is necessary and will make the assembly later on much easier.

Assuming you now have all the pieces you need to build the vanity, and you've verified that all are the correct size, it's a good idea to assemble the casework (without glue) to see how the pieces fit. Using right-angle "C" clamp fixtures, hold all the pieces together (Fig. 4-4). Are all the angles square at the corners? Also, check the overall dimensions: are they the same as your plan calls for? If not, now is the time for taking corrective action.

As you assembled the casework pieces, you no doubt discov-

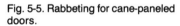
Fig. 5-5. Rabbeting for cane-paneled doors.

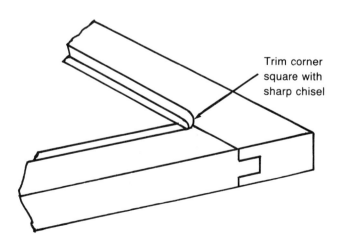
Trim corner square with sharp chisel

ered that certain pieces must be put together before others. Keep this in mind now as you apply glue and begin the final assembly. You might also discover that it's easier to glue two pieces together as subassemblies, let the glue set, and continue on. This approach will require fewer "C" clamps and may initially prove less frustrating. However, when taking this approach be very careful about checking the corner angles. Don't trust the wooden right-angle fixture alone—use your carpenter's or framing square as well.

In drilling for the doweling of the face frame (see Chapter 4), you probably checked to see how the face frame fits. Did you also check its overall dimensions? If not, then reassemble the face frame and verify that it will fit the casework. By proper fit, I mean that with the face frame top lined up flush with the case top, the face frame bottom should cover the bottom of the case. The sides of the face frame should protrude 1/8", unless one end is against a wall, in which case the protrusion should be 1/4".

Chapter 6

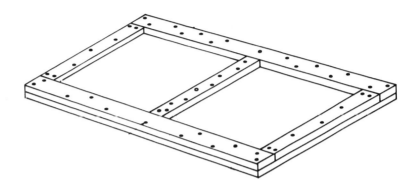

The Finishing Touches

I CANNOT STRESS THE IMPORTANCE OF SANDING ENOUGH. THE novice often assumes that the smooth-planed surface on a board purchased at the lumberyard needs no further finishing because it feels so smooth. If the board is to be used as a closet shelf, then the milled board surface will suffice as is. If it's to become part of a cabinet or piece of furniture, however, sanding will improve the surface tremendously.

SANDING

The role of sanding in the finishing process is often not clearly understood by woodworkers. Frequently, I am asked questions such as: "Will this need sanding?" "How much should I sand it?" "What kind of sandpaper should I use?" "Can I use a power sander?" If you haven't already surmised, some sanding must always be done. Moreover, work that is sanded incorrectly will result in a finish that can never be as fine as it could have been. Let's face it, sanding is work, and it takes time. It's a job that nearly everyone feels is onerous, but it needn't be. Improvements over the years in both equipment and abrasive papers have made it possible for any woodworker to equal or better the work of those meticulous forebears we talked about in the beginning of this book.

As discussed in Chapter 1, sanding can be accomplished with a belt sander, an orbital (pad) sander, and with sanding blocks. In most cases, only the orbital sander is needed to guarantee a professional job. Fast sanding of large, flat surfaces is best done with a belt sander. It does an effective job of sanding new work before assembly, and it is ideal for sanding surfaces with glued up boards. Belt sanders should not be "top heavy," and they should certainly include a vacuum system and dust collection bag. Otherwise, you and your work room will be a mess.

The orbital sander removes unwanted stock rapidly and smoothly through its circular motion. To repeat what was stated in Chapter 1, dual-motion pad sanders are not very useful. An orbital sander will actually cut faster than the in-line motion. Contrary to popular opinion, you need not always sand in the direction of the grain; orbital sanders with sandpaper in the 120- to 320-grit range will not leave circular marks on the wood.

A sanding block can be as simple as a scrap of wood with some sandpaper wrapped around it, or as fancy as a metal holder. I make my own blocks and use scraps of sandpaper left over after cutting out circular pieces for my disc sander. HINT: an old saw blade with the teeth ground off makes a fine disc. If you decide to buy a sanding block, get one with a rubber pad that uses a quarter sheet of sandpaper.

The different methods of grading sandpaper and the generic names used to describe them can be somewhat confusing. When I started working with wood, the only sandpaper available was made with grains of quartz (sand). Today's papers are a vast improvement, beginning with those made with *silicon carbide*, which features high hardness (resistance to wear) and excellent adhesion to the backing. It also resists filling up the grit with wood pulp (*loading*). The most readily available silicon carbide paper is black, sometimes called "wet or dry," and is generally waterproof. It may be used with water or finishing liquids, such as rubbing oil or mineral spirits.

Aluminum oxide paper, which is also widely distributed, has excellent abrasive qualities and is similar in quality to silicon carbide. Some woodworkers feel that silicon carbide, which costs more, is worth the difference. I agree, but only for final finishing or for rubbing varnish or lacquer on fine furniture finish. Most of my sanding is done with aluminum oxide paper. *Garnet* paper, which was once widely used, may be difficult to find without resorting to mail order sources. *Quartz* (sometimes called *flint*) paper is not worth spending your money on, in my opinion; in the long run it will cost more to complete a job than with the higher priced aluminum oxide paper. Table 6-1 shows the various grit numbers and *aughts*.

How does one decide which grit of sandpaper is best to start with? I usually begin with 120-grit, unless the surface is especially rough. If you are hand-sanding, do so with the grain and resist the

Grit No.	Aughts	Description
400	10/0	Very fine
320	9/0	Very fine
280	8/0	Fine
240	7/0	Fine
220	6/0	Fine
180	5/0	Medium
150	4/0	Medium
120	3/0	Medium
100	2/0	Coarse
80	1/0	Coarse
60	1/2	Very coarse
40	1	Very coarse

Table 6-1. Sandpaper Grading.

temptation to sand either in an arc or across the grain. Otherwise, you'll be scratching the wood surface. By sanding across the grain, particularly with the coarser grits, you'll make it all the more difficult to remove those scratches during the final sanding with finer grits. Even though you may think you've sanded out the cross scratches, they are sure to show up when the final finish is applied.

When sanding, a good rule is to skip one grit size after each complete sanding. For example, if the surface has rough spots and you start sanding with 100-grit, switch to 150-grit after all the rough spots have been removed. As a practical matter, the best grits to keep in stock are 80, 100, 120, 220, and 320. You'll never go wrong sanding with too many changes in grit. The idea is to reduce successively the size of each scratch until it can't be seen or felt. Never skip the intermediate step in sanding by going directly from coarse to fine. This holds true whether you're hand-sanding or power-sanding.

To make things easier next time, try using some sanding sticks (Fig. 6-1). Most frequently they measure 5" or 6" long, 3/4" wide, and perhaps a 1/4" thick. These sticks are much like the emery boards women use to file their fingernails. When I'm in a hurry, I merely staple sandpaper onto the stick (but be careful to place the staples where they won't scratch your work). If time permits, use contact bond cement instead to fasten the sandpaper on the stick. The sandpaper may also be bent around one corner of the stick. Try that next time you want to sand both a flat surface and a vertical edge (if only the flat surface needs sanding, then use a stick with sandpaper that goes to the edge of the stick).

Inspecting the finished sanded work in proper light is important. Use a light that can be played across the wood surfaces at a low angle, so that it brings out all the missed dents and scratches. It's worth repeating here that stain and finish won't hide a poor sanding job, they'll only magnify the imperfections. If you're unable to apply the finish right after the final sanding, I recommend resanding with 320-grit just before you apply the finish.

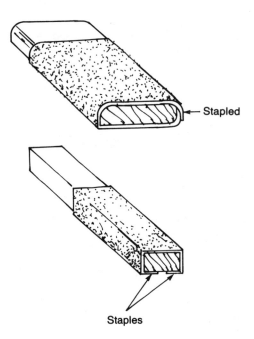

Stapled

Staples

Obviously, it would be easier to sand the cabinet pieces prior to assembly, but care must be taken in that case to avoid rounding the corners. Even when pieces are sanded before assembly, they must be final-sanded after assembly and prior to finishing.

Fig. 6-1. Sanding sticks.

STAINING

Most serious woodworkers, when asked the truth about the art of finishing wood, will tell you they always use "what worked best for them." The specific materials or tools used are frequently less important in achieving fine results than the technique one employs. In other words, the successful woodworker knows how to work *with* the materials, rather than trying to make them act the way he thinks they should. It's important, therefore, to learn what to expect from the materials and what they expect of you. Because you want your cabinetwork to be a quality product that demands a fine finish, don't just jump in with both feet and apply a poor one.

Now is the time to use all those scraps of extra wood you saved, some of which were used for set-ups in the previous cutting processes. Put them to work so you can learn the "feel" of finishing materials without wasting time and material. Try out the finishes you've selected, using scraps of the same wood from which your cabinet is made. Will the stain you've selected hide the grain? Or will it enhance it? If it's the former, thin the stain slightly and try another scrap, keeping track mentally of the proportion of thinner and stain. A word of caution: this process takes time. Allow for it, because stains require time to dry. DO NOT HURRY. You have spent a lot of time making this cabinet—don't ruin it by being too hasty. (One-coat varnish stains are, in my opinion, little better than worthless.)

Does the varnish or lacquer make the underlying stain look "muddy," or does it improve its looks? Will the material you've selected rub out to the desired sheen? I raise these questions not to intimidate you but to make you think seriously about what materials to select. Working with those leftover scraps will help enormously in this regard.

SEALING

I have found that a shellac wash (four parts alcohol to one part shellac) tends to "freeze" the whiskers of wood found on the surface, so that they can be removed more easily with the final sanding. Another good technique is to raise the grain whiskers by wetting the surface with a wet rag or sponge. After the water has been absorbed, pass a propane torch over the surface (being careful not to scorch the surface). When the surface has completely dried, you'll discover a whole forest of whiskers standing up and ready for removal. Make a steel wool ball, using a medium grade, and rub it against the whiskers with the grain until they have disappeared. If you didn't use the first method of removing the whiskers, then you must seal the stain with either the shellac wash or with a carefully laid on thin coat of varnish (one part varnish to two parts thinner or mineral spirits). CAUTION: inspect all visible surfaces to make sure there are no nicks or gouges before sealing or staining. They must be taken care of first.

If, after being so careful, you find a nick or gouge has somehow appeared on the surface, don't despair. There are a number of ways (Fig. 6-2) to patch up such defects with commercial wood fillers, such as plastic wood; sawdust and glue mixture; rub-in crayons; or stick shellac. Depending on location and circumstances, I have use all four of these cures and strongly recommend that you become familiar with them. Let's discuss them, one at a time:

- "Plastic Wood" is best used on surfaces that are not usually visible, such as the back side of a door panel. This method will not take stain very well. It does come in a number of colors but, at best, is difficult to match the final finish color.
- Sawdust and glue mixture is handy, especially when you are working with very fine sawdust. I use it mostly to hide small cracks at joints where the fit isn't as perfect as it might have been. This, too, will not take stain very well, but if the cracks are small enough this should not be noticeable after finishing.
- Rub-in crayons are great when your assembly requires small

finishing nails, and you want to make the nail holes invisible. The crayons, which are found in nearly all hardware stores and lumberyards, come in a multitude of colors that can be mixed on application.

• For really fine work, I usually fall back on stick shellac, which comes in a variety of colors. Stick shellac is not easy to find locally, so you may have to mail-order it from a firm such as Constantine's, which offers a complete assortment of 12 colors for about $24. After carefully cleaning out the gouge or hole, melt the stick shellac into the marred surface with a pencil-type soldering iron (Fig. 6-3). Be careful not to scorch the shellac or it will darken; make sure the shellac is applied above the surface, because it shrinks when it cools. Because stain will not adhere to shellac, use a shellac that matches the final finish.

There is also a produce called *sanding sealer* available at most good paint stores. It is a product that has been available for years, but it seems only professional finishers and cabinetmakers know it exists. It comes in two types; lacquer-based and varnish-based. Depending on the finish you use (probably varnish), purchase the sanding sealer with the same base. *Never* mix bases; otherwise you are asking for a finish that may come apart because it lacks sufficient adherence.

KEEP IT CLEAN

I cannot emphasize enough the importance of a clean shop when applying a finish. Unless you enjoy the luxury of another room in which to apply the finish, I urge you to clean your shop thoroughly, even vacuum it if possible. Why? Because the tiniest particles of dust or lint will end up airborne and find their way to your tacky drying varnish or finish. Subsequent sanding between coats should be only enough to remove the few stray particles that do get on the drying finish. The more particles that stick to your finish, the greater the amount of sanding is required between coats—and the more likelihood you'll cut through the finish and stain right down to the wood. Once again, ''Haste makes waste.''

So spend more time cleaning your shop. It probably could stand a good cleaning anyway after all that machining and sanding. Having done so, sanding between coats should create very little dust,

Fig. 6-3. Melting stick shellac with pencil iron.

and that can be easily removed with a tack cloth (after first wiping with a clean lintless rag).

Once you've cleaned the shop, you're all set to start finishing, right? Wrong! Wait at least 24 hours—until all dust particles have settled. You'll be surprised to find a fine coating of dust on everything, so use your dust cloth on all surfaces close to where you'll do your finishing. Pay particular attention to dusting the floor, because simply by walking around you're bound to stir up more particles.

VARNISHING

Now, at last, you're ready to go. But first, a word about brushes is in order. Another saying is, "You get what you pay for," and it certainly applies to brushes. I have found that a 3" *taper cut* varnish brush is perfect for almost every job. You'll probably have to pay close to $10 for a good one, but it's an excellent investment provided you clean the brush thoroughly after each use. Don't make the mistake of leaving it standing in a can of paint thinner until you need it for the next coat. For one thing, it may take several days before you get around to putting on another coat, and for another, the bristles will get bent, reducing their ability to do a proper job. There's an axiom in finishing that says, "Never use a varnish brush for anything but varnish." You should follow that axiom, because after using a brush for pigmented paint or stain, you'll never remove all the pigment from the brush completely. Some of it will inevitably turn up in your varnished finish as a blemish, ruining hours of hard work.

If you decide to use polyurethane varnish—and I recommend that you do—you'll need to know whether to use satin or gloss. Except on furniture, I use satin, because what's called a "furniture finish" isn't necessary. But please stir the satin varnish thoroughly so that all of the stearate that's settled to the bottom of the can is well mixed. Do not shake a can of varnish; you'll only create air bubbles that can make application even more troublesome. Keep stirring until your mixing paddle is free of stearate.

As you're applying the varnish, shine a bright light across the surface to see those places you've missed. Don't use too much varnish, or you'll create runs or sags. These occur when excess varnish runs down a vertical surface and "piles up." After you've finished varnishing the cabinet, be sure to look for pile-ups and brush out the excess before it dries.

How long should you wait between coats? Follow the directions, which usually recommend 24 hours. But don't wait too long, like a week, because the next coat will not adhere as well. My rule of thumb is 12 to 24 hours after sealing, 24 hours after the first coat, and 24 hours after the second coat. If a third coat is used, I suggest waiting 48 hours before applying it.

It's essential that you sand lightly between each coat. Otherwise, you'll create what looks like tiny mountains and valleys. The object of applying several coats of finish is to fill those valleys with varnish or finish. Be especially careful to control your sanding, particularly on the first coat, so that you do not sand through the finish. Upon completion of each sanding operation, carefully wipe the surface with a tack cloth, periodically folding in the corners as the cloth accumulates dust and lint.

COUNTERTOPS

Countertops can be made two ways (as shown in Figs. 6-4 and 6-5). You can use 3/4-inch thick underlayment plywood, or particle board that is specially made for countertops. I don't recommend using regular particle board for the *banded* method (Fig. 6-4), because it is not as strong as the 25-inch wide special particle board. In both types, the countertop should overhang the cabinet by an inch on the exposed sides (unless the cabinet is in a corner, in which case the countertop overhangs two sides). If the cabinet is a base unit located next to a refrigerator, the countertop overhang should be eliminated.

One advantage of using the alternate method (Fig. 6-5) is that the countertop can be fabricated as one large piece, using stiffeners to join pieces of particle board. A disadvantage is that the stiffeners must be perfectly flush with the exposed edges, which will later be covered by Formica.

When cutting plywood or particle board (I prefer the latter), use a carbide-tipped blade. How do you cut a straight line when cutting a large sheet with a power saw? Figure 6-6 shows a piece of pine tacked to the large sheet. The pine is offset from the cutline

Fig. 6-4. Banded countertop substrate is applied to edge.

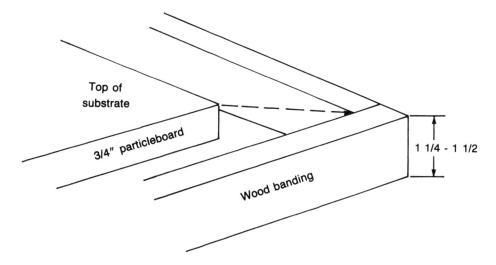

Top of substrate

3/4" particleboard

Wood banding

1 1/4 - 1 1/2

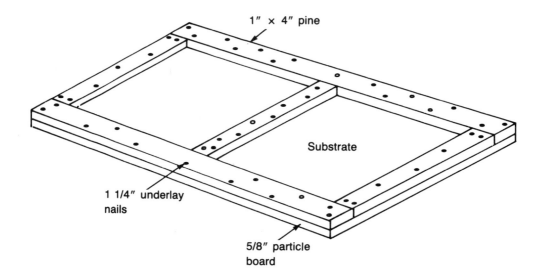

1" × 4" pine

Substrate

1 1/4" underlay
nails

5/8" particle
board

the same distance as from the sawblade to the saw's sole or baseplate. By tacking the pine along a snapped chalk line, you should get a perfectly straight cut. When measuring and marking particle board, allow extra width and length so that you can scribe it (Fig. 6-7) for a perfect fit to the wall. Cut a rabbet on the sides against the walls to make the scribing easier.

If you decide to use the banded countertop method, and the banding is to be covered by plastic laminate (Formica), it can be made with pine or softwood. Rip sufficient stock to the desired band width (usually 1 1/2") and cut all the required pieces to length. Then using 6d nails glue the bands to the particle board. When gluing along the edge of particle board, I recommend that the glue be applied twice because of the board's porosity. Apply one coat, let it

Fig. 6-5. Reinforced countertop from bottom view.

Fig. 6-6. Cutting a straight line on large plywood.

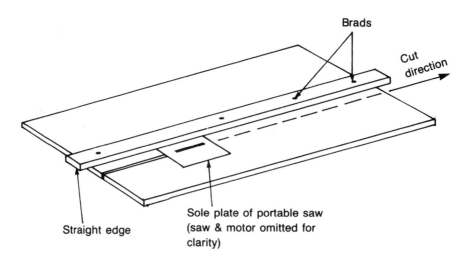

Brads

Cut
direction

Straight edge

Sole plate of portable saw
(saw & motor omitted for
clarity)

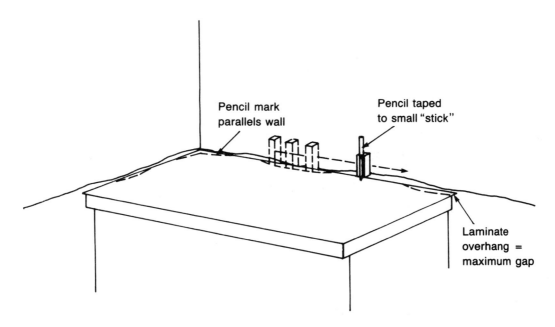

Fig. 6-7. Scribing countertop.

soak in, and then apply another coat as you nail the banding to the edge.

When the banding glue has dried, plane or sand the banding flush with the top surface of the particle board. Take care not to bevel or round the banding; otherwise the laminate won't be properly supported.

With the scribing and banding complete, it's now time to glue the Formica or plastic laminate to the top. For this task you will need contact adhesive, a 2-inch throw-away brush, and enough sticks to lay across the countertop every foot or so. The sticks should be about 1/4″ square. If your doors were made 3/8″ offset, you should have enough 1/4″ pieces left over from cutting the doors to fit. If not, cut some scrap boards 24″ to 30″ long and rip them to 1/4″ square.

When ordering or buying plastic laminates, allow sufficient footage to provide for the edging you'll need. The widths usually available are 24″, 30″, 36″, and 48″. Standard lengths are 6′, 8′, 10′, and 12′. If you need smaller pieces, ask the dealer if he has any scraps, or if he'll sell you some smaller pieces. The dealer who supplies you with plastic laminate will also have the proper contact adhesive. *Do not* use water based contact cement. I have found that it results in unsatisfactory adhesion and seems to take forever to dry.

Make sure that you perform the contact cement job in a well ventilated place, because it is highly volatile. Coat all edges of the countertop and laminate twice. When the cement is dry to the touch, carefully locate one laminate edge strip and press it into place (Fig.

Labels in figure:
Pencil mark parallels wall
Pencil taped to small "stick"
Laminate overhang = maximum gap

6-8). *Once the top makes contact with the laminate, you will not be able to remove it!*

Because you are making your own top, you probably own a router or have access to one. In either case, you must acquire a carbide laminate cutter to do the trimming. You must also have a flat bastard file to break the finished sharp edges. After each edge piece is pressed in place, trim it with the router. On the ends, where the edge strips overlap, carefully file and end flush with the edge. Continue this operation until all edges have plastic laminate applied. None is needed along the edges that abut walls.

Before gluing the top piece of laminate, be sure that all of the edging is flush with the top. If is isn't, you won't get proper ding. Also, check to see if there's a crack between the edging and the substrate. If so, was it because the laminate wasn't pressed into the contact cement? Or was the top edge sanded or installed improperly? Fill any minor gaps with Elmer's wood putty before proceeding.

Now you're ready to glue the top laminate to the countertop. Again, in a well ventilated area, spread or paint the contact adhesive, first on the back side of the laminate and then on the particle board. Even though most contact cement cans advise one coat, I suggest applying two coats. When both surfaces are dry to touch, it's time to apply the laminate to the countertop substrate. First place several 1/4" square sticks across the countertop substrate about every 12" (as done on one edge in Fig. 6-8). Then lay the laminate on top of the sticks and carefully align it so that some material hangs over each edge. Carefully pull out the first stick at one end and press the laminate down until it adheres to the top. Make sure the laminate is still straight and continue pulling out the sticks one at a time, pressing the laminate down on the substrate. When all the sticks have been removed, take a scrap block of wood and

Fig. 6-8. Gluing laminate edge.

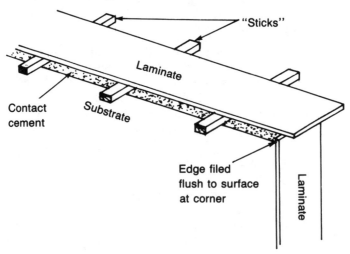

"Sticks"

Laminate

Contact cement

Substrate

Edge filed
flush to surface
at corner

Laminate

move it over the whole top, hammering lightly as you go. This will assure a firm set for the contact adhesive and also remove any bubbles that may have formed.

The final step is to remove the overhanging laminate. Here again, the router with its carbide cutter and roller guide should remove the surplus without difficulty. When all surplus is removed, it's a good idea to break the sharp edges with a file held at 45°. Run the file once over all corners and edges.

Chapter 7

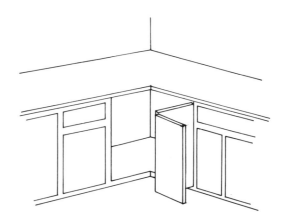

Drawers, Doors,
Shelves, and Hardware

Y OU'VE PROBABLY ALREADY NOTICED THAT THERE ARE many ways to make cabinet drawers. A typical drawer is shown in Fig. 7-1. In the early days, a drawer was simply a box that slid on wooden rails fastened to the cabinet sides. Drawers of higher quality also had a center guide, which is usually found in good furniture as part of the *dust panel* (a dust panel is essentially a cover to prevent dust or dirt from traveling downward from drawer to drawer).

DRAWER CONSTRUCTION

Traditionally, drawers were usually made out of hardwood, because the drawer bottom acted as a slide; thus, wear was an important consideration. Nowadays nearly all drawers, except in fine furniture, use metal or plastic slides of one sort or another instead of hardwood. Figure 7-2 shows the most common types of drawer corner construction.

Installing The Slides

The first step in constructing a drawer is to decide what type of drawer slide to use. Aside from using the drawer itself as part of the slide (not recommended), there are two types of commercially available slides. The best (and most expensive) slide mounts on each

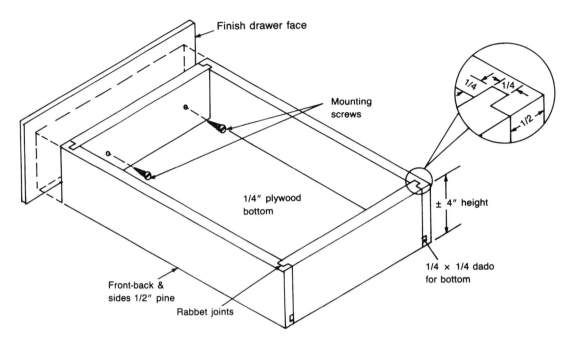

Finish drawer face

Mounting screws

1/4" plywood bottom

± 4" height

1/4 × 1/4 dado for bottom

Front-back & sides 1/2" pine

Rabbet joints

1/4   1/4   1/2

Fig. 7-1. Typical cabinet drawer.

side of the drawer and cabinet. It's most often found on custom made furniture of the highest quality. That's because, in part, it requires more precision in mounting than the center-mount-type.

The center-mount-type uses a center guide system in combination with rollers mounted on the bottom drawer rail of the cabinet face frame. I strongly recommend using this type because it can be easily mounted, performs very well, and is modest in cost. The directions found in any good commercial drawer slide will indicate how much smaller than the face frame opening the drawer must be. Therefore, I suggest that you procure the slides before making the drawers. When purchasing the slides, you'll discover they come in a variety of lengths. The length you need is determined by measuring the distance from the inside back of the cabinet to the front of the face frame. Some slides require you to cut the track to exact length with a hacksaw, so read the directions carefully before buying, and make sure you return the slides if they are the wrong length.

Because of its cost and ease of use, what I will describe here is a drawer built to use with a single-track, under-drawer slide. Most of those slides are available only in 22 5/8" lengths, but don't be concerned. If the slide you've bought is too long, you can simply cut the track to the desired length. Such a slide should meet the requirements of any household drawer: it fits any length of width of drawer, and it will handle loads up to 50 pounds. One manufacturer, Knape and Vogt, claims that no measuring, marking, or templates are required. That claim may be oversimplified; it usually

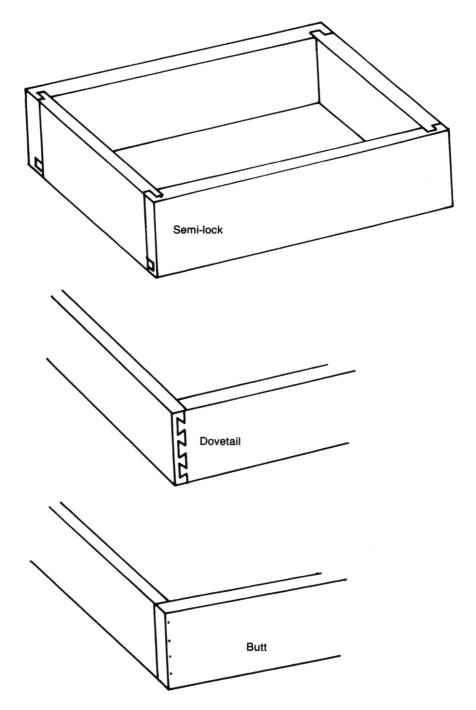

Semi-lock

Dovetail

Butt

Fig. 7-2. Types of common drawer corner joints.

pays to measure and locate the rear support so that it is centered in the back of the cabinet case and at the proper height. Likewise, the roller mounted on the back of the drawer should be centered, so measuring is required there too. In general, however, these slides are relatively easy to install, are well made, and operate efficiently.

Now that the slides are in, and you've decided to use the single track system, you need only to decide how much clearance is required between the drawer sides and the stiles (the ones that form the drawer opening on the cabinet face frame). An 1/8″ clearance all the way around the drawer is usually acceptable, and a bit more certainly won't hurt. The height and width of the drawer will therefore be at least 1/4″ less than the opening itself (1/8″ × 2). When you measure the opening, you'll probably discover that it's not the exact dimension you planned. Not to worry. Simply subtract 1/4″ from whatever the measurement. If either dimension has to be read in 1/16″ increments, use a dimension that is the nearest 1/8″ below that figure. For example, we have used a width measurement of 13 15/16″. By subtracting 1/4″ that leaves 13 11/16″, so the final width becomes 13 5/8″. The drawer height, which is less critical, normally measures 1/2″ less than the opening; this helps prevent jamming of the drawer's contents (utensils, silverware, etc.) upon closing. The depth of the drawer is almost always 1 1/2″ less than the cabinet depth. This allows for the use of hardware—usually a part of the drawer slides—which must also be taken into consideration.

The Materials List

Once again, a materials list (Table 7-1) is in order to ensure that all necessary lumber is at hand in order to cut the needed parts. Table 7-1 indicates a need for 1/2″ drawer slides. I have used 3/4″ stock, but it's too massive and looks amateurish, so I recommend buying 1/2″ pine for the drawers. The bottoms can be made with 1/4″ plywood or tempered masonite. If 1/4″ plywood was used for the case back, there are probably enough leftover scraps to use for the drawer bottoms. If the plywood scrap is close to the size you need—but not exactly so—you may want to adjust the drawer dimensions slightly so that it can be used. That's where the importance of planning comes in; it enables you to adjust all dimensions to utilize available materials to the fullest.

Dividers

There's one last consideration: do you want built-in dividers (Figs.

Table 7-1. Drawers Materials List.

Label	Qty	Description	Size
DF	4	Drawer front & back	1/2 ″ × 4″ × 12 5/8″
DS	4	Drawer sides	1/2″ × 4″ × 18″
DB	2	Drawer bottoms	1/4″ × 17″ × 12 1/8″

Fig. 7-3. Drawer dividers help keep contents neat.

Fig. 7-4. Dividers installed in kitchen drawers.

7-3 and 7-4)? If so, it will be necessary to *dado* (groove) the sides, and possibly the front and back as well, depending on how the drawer is divided. The dados should be very shallow (1/8″) to avoid weakening the sides. Leftover plywood can also be used for the dividers, in which case the dado should be 1/4″ wide and 1/8″ deep (Fig. 7-5).

A quick but less elegant way to install drawer dividers is to use *zip clips* which provide ready-made grooves. Measuring up to 1/4″ in thickness and 1 3/4″ in length, these channel-shaped steel supports are installed without screws or nails. Sharp prongs on the back of each clip make it easy to tap the clips in place in the wood. Mail order firms such as Constantine's can supply them.

Careful preplanning of drawers is essential in making dividers. The grooves (Fig. 7-6) into which the dividers slide must be cut in the drawer walls prior to assembly. The dividers themselves may be 1/4″ or 1/2″ plywood, depending on their length and use. Regular kitchen drawers should be made with 1/2″ thick wood. If cross dividers are desired, they must be notched line "egg crates" as shown in Fig. 7-7. Sanding the plywood divider edges will suffice, but a better way is to band the exposed edges with thin wood

Fig. 7-5. Dividers slide into drawer.

Fig. 7-6. Note grooves routed out in dividers.

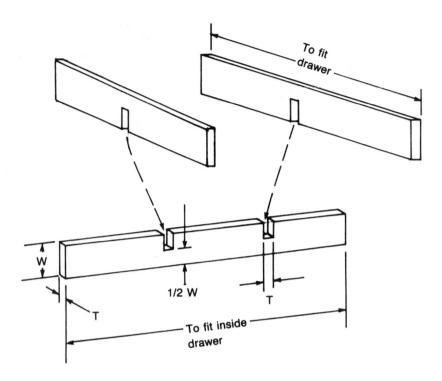

Fig. 7-7. Divider details.

strips. this is not a difficult task and will improve appearances tremendously.

The process of banding dividers is the same as discussed in the section on shelves; however, if the bands are very thin—1/16" to 1/8"—clamping isn't necessary. Use masking tape to hold the strips on until the glue dries. Remember, the strips should be wider than the divider thickness, so that after drying they can be sanded flush. In cutting all the material for the cabinet face and doors (Chapters 3 and 4), we included pieces labeled "drawer fronts." These pieces do not refer to the front of the drawers; rather they are pieces that screw onto the drawer box itself to hide the gap between the drawer and the face frame. I recommend fastening the finish drawer face at the very end, after all finishing is completed. That way, you can line up all the faces, one to the other, so that they look perfect when closed (even though the drawers may not be). If there's to be a "fake" drawer front, such as on a sink where the installation of a drawer is prohibited, it should be mounted with cleats (see Fig. 7-8).

DOORS

A board-and-batten door is sometimes used when a rustic look is desired. Frequently, the doors are made from 6" knotty pine tongue and groove boards held together with battens screwed into the rear

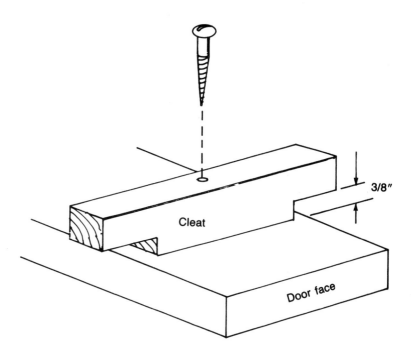

3/8"

Cleat

Door face

Fig. 7-8. Cleats for false drawer fronts.

of the door. This type of door is usually a full overlap on the face frame.

Among the several different methods for hanging doors on cabinets or furniture, these are the most popular:

- *Full-overlay.* This means that the full thickness of the door overlaps the opening of the face frame. It's the most common method used in kitchen cabinets that are European or contemporary in style. Full-overlay doors use concealed hinges, such as Grass, which are known throughout the world as the finest made. They are six-way adjustable; hence door installation and adjustment are easily accomplished. This type of hinge is more expensive than either cabinet or pivot types.
- *Half-overlay.* This means that half the thickness of the door overlaps the face frame opening. It is perhaps the most widely used method of hanging doors in both cabinets and furniture. The door edges are rabbeted around the outside edge to form a lip, which frequently is molded or rounded. Hinges for this type of door hanging must have one leaf of the hinge offset 3/8" to allow for mounting the hinge to the lip. The Grass-type hinge is also available for this type of mounting.
- *Inset or flush hanging.* In this method, the surface of the door is flush with the surface of the face frame. This system, which is most frequently found in fine furniture, is rarely used in cabinetry, perhaps because with heavy usage it tends to get out of adjustment,

or because it takes more time and craftsmanship to create proper fits. In any case, I do not recommend this method for the amateur cabinetmaker. Figure 7-9 shows the construction of a typical cabinet door.

Hardware

Hinges and drawer-door pulls come in an almost endless variety of styles and finishes. When you select your hinges and pulls, they should be in keeping with the style of door. Do not, for instance, buy pivot hinges for an overlay door when you plan to build half overlap or inset doors.

I recommend that all hinges and drawer slides be mounted prior to finishing the cabinet. If any adjustments or modifications are necessary it is far easier to make them before applying the finish. Frequently, when hinges are mounted by measuring from an edge and then installed on the face frame, later adjustments will pull the knobs out of line. Precision may be important, but appearance is

Fig. 7-9. Typical cabinet door.

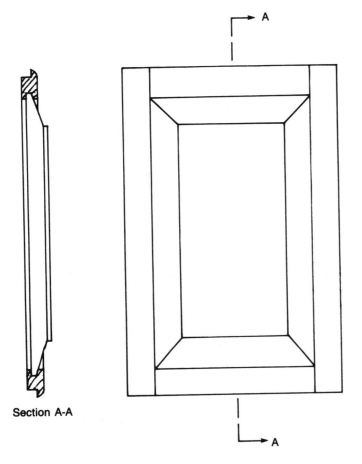

Section A-A

A

A

what finally counts. It may seem like unnecessary work to mount all the hardware (except pulls and knobs) and then remove them during the finishing process, but it's better than taking a chance on marring your fine finish by slipping with a drill or awl.

When attaching hinges or other hardware, take care to center the pilot holes. If you are careless, the off-center holes can cause the hinge to bind. Locate the hinges from the top and bottom of the door with a scrap of wood used as a gauge (Fig. 7-10); then, with a sharp pencil, draw around the mounting hole. In soft wood, I use a sharp awl to create a centered pilot hole; with hardwood, you should use drill a drill.

Now, with the casework lying on its back, place all the doors on the cabinet face. Assuming that you are mounting doors that are half-overlap (3/8" lip) with no center stiles, check each door or pair of doors to make sure there is about 1/8" play within the face frame. If binding occurs, now is the time to take corrective action. Determine where the door binds, and set up the saw so that the blade protrudes slightly less than 3/8". Set the rip fence so that it is 3/8" away from the near face of the saw blade. After removing the hinges, pass the door through the saw, and you will widen the lip on the door by the thickness of the saw blade. Remount the hinges and recheck the fit, if there is still binding, with the same saw setting, pass the opposite lip through the saw.

Catches

One good way to keep the doors on your cabinets closed is with a *bullet catch*, which is spring-loaded and looks like a bullet. It's used most often in conjunction with an elbow catch and strike on furniture, where two doors close together without a stile between them. Until recently, various types of magnetic catches were most

Fig. 7-10. Scrap wood gauge for mounting hinges.

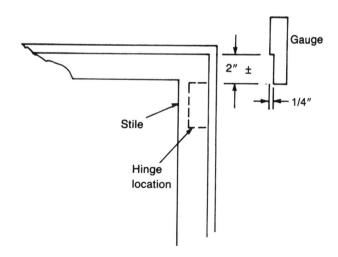

often used on cabinets. One of their major disadvantages, however, is that they are difficult to mount and keep in adjustment. Many hinges now are of the self-closing-type, which eliminates the catch because the door is held shut by the hinge. A self-closing hinge is easy to install, requires no adjustment, and is actually less expensive than a conventional hinge and catch.

Another useful latch system is the *Tutch Latch*, which opens cabinet doors automatically at a gentle touch of the finger, arm, or elbow. It is designed especially for use on wooden cabinets, but it has many other applications as well. Its design ensures a positive latching action, whether the door is slammed or closed gently. Installation is relatively easy. A magnetic version of this latch is also available. You may be able to find most of these latches in lumberyards and hardware stores, but others may have to be bought by mail.

SHELVING

Many space-saving improvements can be added to your cabinets to improve their usefulness and efficiency. A trip to the hardware or variety store will reveal a nearly endless array of such items, such as a convenient disappearing pan rack that can be simply and quickly fastened in a cabinet to improve space utilization. Others include a sliding towel rack for keeping towels out of sight under the sink, a cookbook rack that folds away when not in use, spice racks, and door shelves. You'll also find mixer shelf designed to swing a small appliance shelf up out of the cabinets and lock it securely at a convenient working height.

Revolving shelves for corner cabinets are also available. I try to discourage the use of base cabinets with revolving shelves because I feel they waste too much space. Less than half the space is available for use with 24″ revolving shelves (Figs. 7-11 and 7-12), so, when making corner cabinets, consider making them with shelves and a double hinged door (Fig. 7-13) to give the greatest access. Revolving shelves on wall cabinets are useful because they bring everything up front with less space wasted. Hardware for either wall or base cabinets is readily available and easily installed. If you do plan to use this type of hardware, I recommend that you obtain it prior to construction of the cabinets. That way, you won't design yourself into a corner where the shelves won't fit.

Shelving Materials

Shelving can be made from either wood or particle board. Shelves in most moderate-cost commercial cabinets are made of high density particle board covered with a simulated wood grain veneer. When you visit the lumberyard, you'll find that they probably carry

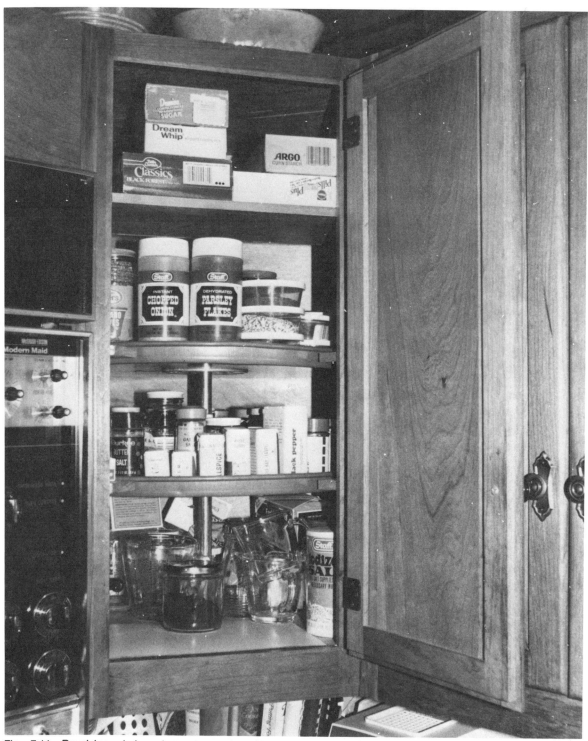

Fig. 7-11. Revolving shelves in upper corner cabinet.

Fig. 7-12. Revolving shelves in lower cabinet.

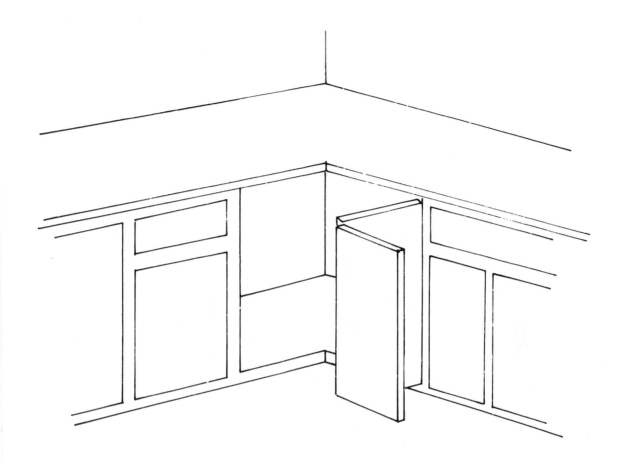

Fig. 7-13. Hinged corner door.

two types of particle board—shelving and countertop grades, which are 3/4″ thick with high density, and 48″ × 96″ sheets in various thicknesses with low density. I do not recommend using the low density particle board. It is structurally weaker and absorbs moisture readily. Shelves made of low density particle board will inevitably warp in time. Because you will no doubt lack the means for applying a veneer to the particle board, I suggest you band at least the long edges with wood. This will not only improve the looks of the edges, it will stiffen the shelves and minimize possible warping. NOTE: when cutting particle board with a saw, bear in mind that it is very abrasive and rapidly dulls regular blades, so use a carbide blade to cut it.

A better choice of materials for cabinet shelves is, in my opinion, plywood. Unless the shelves are small or will not have to carry much weight, I'd recommend a 5/8″ or 3/4″ thickness. Shelves that are 1/2″ thick will work in wall cabinets only when the shelf length is 18″ or less.

When purchasing plywood for your cabinets, it's wise to pay a bit more for five-ply birch veneer, which offers a far superior finish than does fir plywood. Do not use three-ply plywood except for backs or drawer bottoms. It is difficult to finish the edges with banding, and it is not as strong structurally. Again, banding should be applied to all edges of the plywood.

Shelves can also be made from solid wood boards. Common pine is perfectly satisfactory for shelves, but be sure to select boards with tight knots and growth rings that run all the way through the board. This will minimize twisting and warping. Select, knot-free lumber is the most expensive solution to shelves. Another possibility is glued-up shelving stock; it's knot free and its cost is somewhere between select lumber and No. 2 common.

When making the finish cuts to the exact shelving dimensions required, make the cross cuts first. Cross cutting first allows the ripping operation to cut off the splinters created in cross cutting. If you do not have sufficient stock to rip both sides off, place some scrap stock behind the work. Also, because the saw blade tears slightly as it exits the cut, keep the finish side up.

Banding

Because the edges of plywood and particle board are rough and ugly, they need to be covered. One way to do this is with wood tape, which is a thin (1/32" thick) strip of wood 3/4" or more in width. It comes in rolls. Some wood tape already has adhesive on one side and is either pressure or heat sensitive, so it can be ironed on. If there's wood tape available that uses glue, contact cement can be used instead. Be sure to double coat both the tape and the rough edge to be covered so that a good bond is achieved.

If there's no ready source of tape, you can cut your own, as I do. Banding particle board or plywood is a simple procedure really. The wood strips you cut for the bands must be slightly thicker than the material being banded. The width of the band can vary. (I use 1/2" to 3/4" on shelves and 1/8" on plywood.) When ripping your banding stock, you'll need a *pusher stick*. Also, when ripping the material to the correct width, remember to allow for the banding. That means the plywood or particle board must be narrower to compensate for the bands. On both plywood and particle board, it's important to get a good glue joint to ensure that the bands don't come off. Because the edges of plywood and particle board are very porous, I spread glue on them first and let it soak in for 10 to 15 minutes, then spread more glue on the edge as the bands are applied.

Figure 7-14 shows how edge banding is done using pipe clamps. Before setting aside the banded shelves to dry, recheck the banding so that it doesn't slip while clamping. The band should be slightly raised on each side to allow sanding or planing to a perfect finish and flush with the shelf surface. Do not try to sand

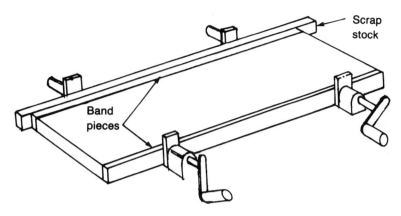

Fig. 7-14. Edge banding.

or plane the bands flush until the glue is thoroughly dry, however, but wait until the next day. Sanding the bands flush is best done with a belt sander, because other sanders will tend to round the corners. A hand plane will give excellent results, but be sure to rest as much of the plane sole on the shelf surface as possible. Now carefully move the plane parallel to the glue line so that it doesn't dig into the shelf surface. This will help avoid beveling the band (see Fig. 7-15).

HINT: you may occasionally find that the material at hand is a bit too narrow to use. You can widen it by simply gluing a band to it.

Supports

Shelves may be supported in a number of ways. Perhaps the simplest is through the use of *cleats,* which are usually found in closets. They are particularly effective when the shelf is very long, because the back cleat helps support the entire length of the shelf. Sometimes shelves can become an integral part of the cabinet by being set in dadoes (see Fig. 7-16). This method is an excellent choice where there is no need to change shelf heights, because it makes an incredibly strong and permanent cabinet.

With shelves that must be adjustable, two common methods of support are used. The simplest and least expensive way is to

Fig. 7-15. Planing bands.

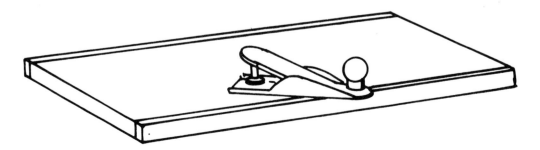

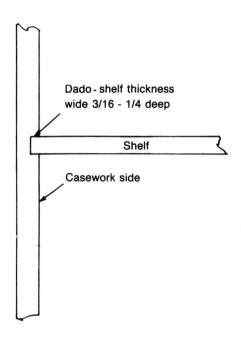

Dado - shelf thickness
wide 3/16 - 1/4 deep

Shelf

Casework side

use shelf brackets like those shown in Fig. 7-17. Start by drilling a series of 1/4″ holes on each side of the cabinet walls for the bracket. The trick here is to make sure each set of holes is equidistant from the bottom of the cabinet. Figure 4-10 shows a simple jig that ensures that all holes match once they are drilled. This method of support is most commonly found in kitchen and vanity cabinets with adjustable shelves.

Another shelf support method uses *standards*, which are metal tracklike pieces with slits spaced 1/2″ apart into which special support brackets are placed. These may be either flush or surface

Fig. 7-16. Shelves in dadoes.

Fig. 7-17. Shelf bracket.

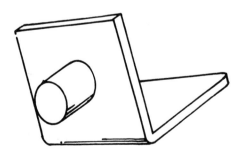

mounted to the cabinet side wall. Bookcases almost always have shelves supported in this manner. A variation of this method is often used for mounting shelves on a wall where no side members exist, but it is not considered suitable for cabinets.

Chapter 8

Wall and Pantry Cabinets

T HE CONSTRUCTION OF WALL CABINETS IS SIMILAR TO OUR description of building and designing base cabinets (Chapter 2). Once again, we need to make up sketches and materials lists, which will be similar to those used for base cabinets. Before making your drawings and lists, however, decide whether you want fixed shelves or movable ones. Movable shelves will allow for the addition or deletion of shelves later on, whereas fixed ones won't.

WALL CABINETS

Wall cabinets are made with two structural members not found in base cabinets. The cross section of a typical wall cabinet (Fig. 8-1) shows the top and bottom mounting rails, which become the structural parts of the cabinet. When screwed into the wall studs, these rails will provide sufficient weight support. Note the mounting rails are rabbeted to allow for flush-mounting the plywood back. The mounting rails may also be set into the back, where they are covered by the plywood, thus eliminating the rabbeting operation, which requires a bigger piece of plywood. Either way, there is no structural difference in installing the mounting rails. If any of the wall cabinet ends are exposed, remember to increase the length of the exposed side so its bottom matches the face frame bottom.

Cabinets with removable shelves longer than 36″ are not

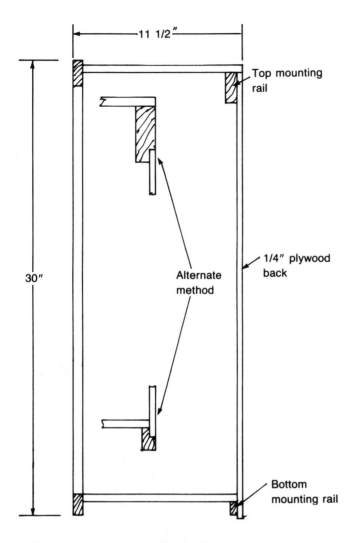

11 1/2"

30"

Top mounting
rail

1/4" plywood
back

Alternate
method

Bottom
mounting rail

Fig. 8-1. Wall cabinet mounting rails.

desirable unless there is a center shelf support to prevent sagging. To provide for center supports when an extra wide cabinet is required—say 48"—install a vertical stile between the top and bottom mounting rails at the back center of the cabinet. This stile, along with a counterpart on the face frame, will provide enough support for shelving as well. The stile on the face frame is called a *meeting stile*, because that's where the doors meet. A 48" cabinet will, in all probability, end up with four doors, so make the center stile of the face frame wide enough to allow space for both sets of hinges.

The wall cabinet shown in Fig. 8-2 is used as an example in creating the materials list shown in Table 8-1. If your design needs are wider or narrower, adjust the dimensions accordingly.

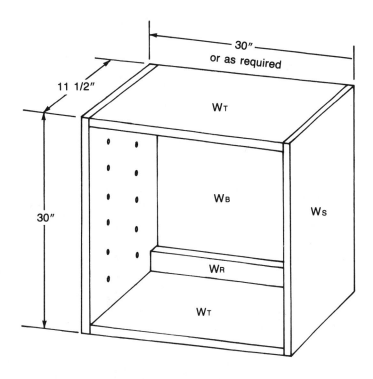

Fig. 8-2. Wall cabinet labels.

Table 8-1. Wall Cabinet Materials List.

PANTRY CABINETS

Before you create a design for your pantry cabinets, spend some time looking at the various organizers that are available. If you'd like to adopt some of those ideas, either purchase the organizers ready-made or write down the measurements so that you can design your pantry cabinet around them. Would shelves on the door improve things? One way to provide them is to purchase an available unit and mount it on the pantry door; another is to make the door like that shown in Fig. 8-3. In either case, the load on ordinary hinges will be excessive, so use a piano hinge along the entire length of the door. Piano hinges should be readily available in the

Label	Qty	Description	Size
WT	2	Top and bottom	1/2" × 11 1/2" × 29"
WS	2	Sides	1/2" × 11 1/2" × 30"
WB	1	Back*	1/4" × 29" × 29 1/2"
WR	2	Support rails	3/4" × 29" × 3 1/2"

* Assumes the support rails are set inside back with the top, bottom and sides rabbeted 1/4" × 1/4" for the back.

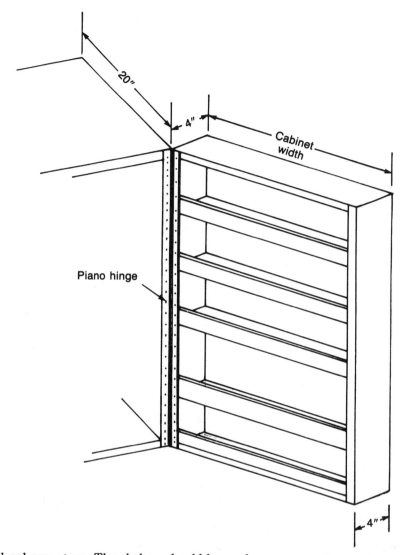

Fig. 8-3. Pantry door shelves.

lumberyard or hardware store. The shelves should be made as a structural unit using 1/2″ plywood. Don't forget to put either a lip or a dowel across the shelf to prevent objects from falling off. The finished door is then attached to the back.

The pantry door shown, which is 4″ deep, would actually be the front portion of the cabinet, which is 24″, leaving 20″. In effect, you are building a cabinet that's a closed box with a front and a back and then cutting off the front 4″ (or deeper if you prefer) to make the door. If the kitchen layout won't permit this arrangement, then the door must become a part of the structure with the piano hinges mounted to it. The shelves must then be made narrow enough to clear the side wall of the cabinet when the door is opened.

DRAWER TRAYS

Drawer trays installed in a few of the cabinet drawers will increase the storage space in a drawer and allow easier access to the contents of the drawer. Usually, drawer trays are relatively shallow and are about half the length of the drawer. Hardwood rails (1/4″ × 1/2″ × inside drawer length) are screwed to the drawer sides, allowing the tray to be pushed back for easy access to contents at the bottom of the drawer.

The most useful drawer tray I've found is one mounted in a drawer under the corner of a peninsula counter. It, along with the cabinet underneath, uses the otherwise lost space of a blind corner (see Fig. 8-4). Notice that the drawer pulls out past the 1/4″ overhang of the countertop, due to the double extension drawer slides. The drawer contains phone books, with note paper and pencils in the tray that are always out of the way but handy for use at the phone.

The tray shown in the picture was made from 1/4″ birch plywood. It is not necessary to nail or screw the parts together; a proper gluing job will do the trick. I've found that pregluing all the bottom edges and ends and then recoating with glue a second time makes a very strong assembly. Masking tape at the corners,

Fig. 8-4. Drawer tray.

as shown in Fig. 8-5, works well in holding all the parts together while they dry. If you want to dress up the tray, band the top edges of the plywood and use a 45° miter at the corners.

CUTTING BOARDS

Cutting boards can be built in the base cabinets two ways: by using a slot above the drawer opening; or inside a drawer mounted on rails like a tray. Cutting boards should be made by laminating birch strips with a waterproof glue. When finished, it will look like a small chopping board. Before you go to the trouble of making a cutting board, though, you may discover that a good, inexpensive one can be bought at a variety store or unfinished-furniture store. Either adjust the drawer and cabinet to fit a stock size or cut a larger one down to the required size.

If you decide that a large cutting board is needed, then it's probably best to put a slot in the face frame and mount it directly under the countertop. Rails must be made at the top of the base cabinet to accommodate the breadboard, along with a stop to prevent it from being pushed in too far. The stop is made with a short length of 1/4″ dowel glued in a hole at the proper distance from the front. The front member of the top frame (see Fig. 2-8) must be removed to allow enough room for the breadboard to slide under the countertop (the modification will look like Fig. 8-6).

WINE RACK

If your kitchen frequently serves as a bar, you'll want some space for a wine rack. The wind rack cabinet casework is the same as

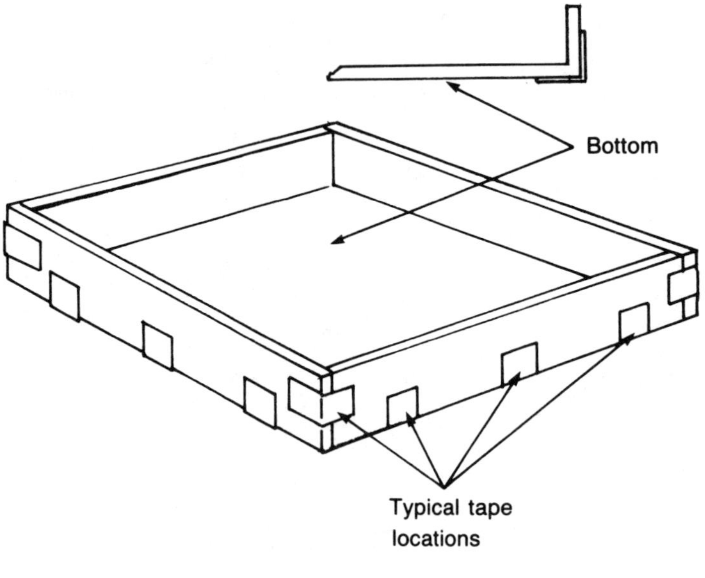

Fig. 8-5. Gluing tray with tape clamps.

Bottom

Typical tape locations

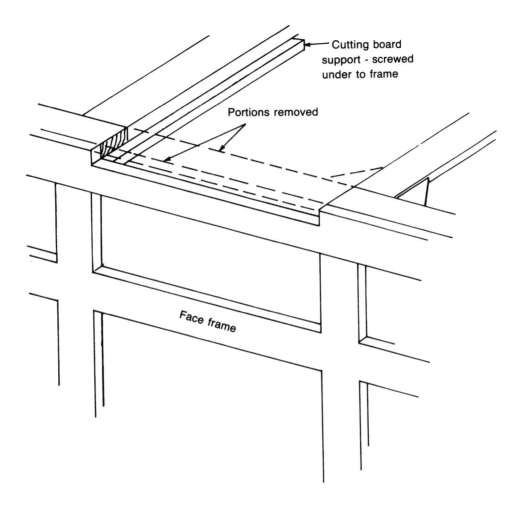

Cutting board support - screwed under to frame

Portions removed

Face frame

Fig. 8-6. Face frame modification for breadboard.

other wall cabinets, but care must be taken to ensure that the mounting rails are well fastened. The bottle holders, which act as inserts in the cabinet, can be constructed in one or two basic ways, depending on one's taste. Horizontal bars with "V" notches or a semicircular cut (such as sketched in Fig. 8-7) is one method, and lattice-work is the other. The lattice-work probably looks better, but it's more difficult to build (see Fig. 8-8 for construction details). Lattice construction will be simpler if it's made oversize and then trimmed to fit the casework. You'll need two sets, so be sure to cut duplicates of all the pieces. Trying to measure for each cut is a tedious process and will probably not yield satisfactory results. Figure 8-9 shows how to make precision cut dadoes or notches that are equally spaced.

The layout for cutting lattice-work to its final size is quite simple. Find the intersection of the lattice pieces nearest the center and draw a vertical line through them. Using one-half the inside

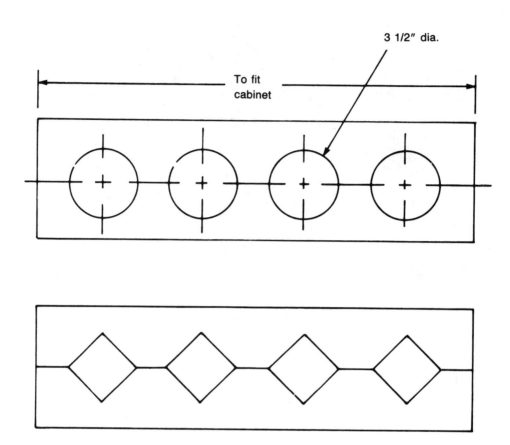

3 1/2" dia.

To fit cabinet

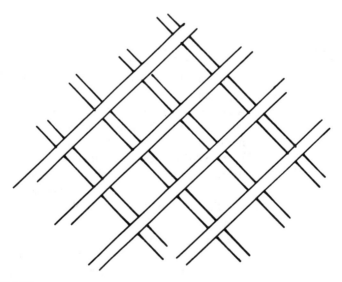

Fig. 8-7. Wine rack support bars.

Fig. 8-8. Wine rack lattice.

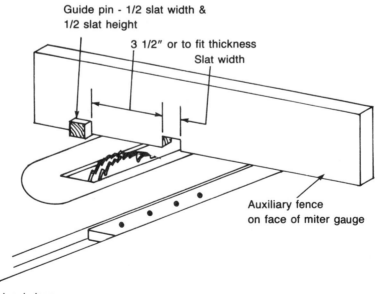

Guide pin - 1/2 slat width &
1/2 slat height

3 1/2" or to fit thickness

Slat width

Auxiliary fence
on face of miter gauge

Fig. 8-9. Fixture for spacing dadoes.

cabinet width, mark either side of the vertical center line at both the top and bottom of the lattice. By drawing a line between those marks, you will arrive at the proper cut line for the sides. To find where the top and bottom cuts should be made, repeat the process with a horizontal center line. This time, make your marks on the center line. Use a framing square lined up with one of the side lines to draw the top and bottom line through the marks on the vertical center line (Fig.8-10).

GLASS HOLDER

Glass holders can add a finishing touch to your wine rack and can

Fig. 8-10. Final sizing of lattice.

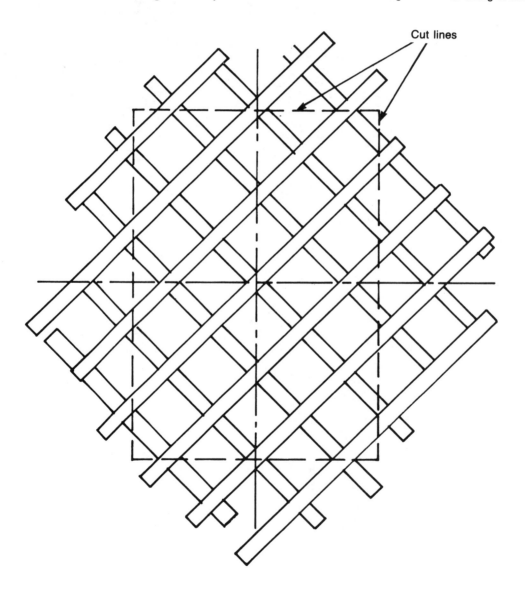

Cut lines

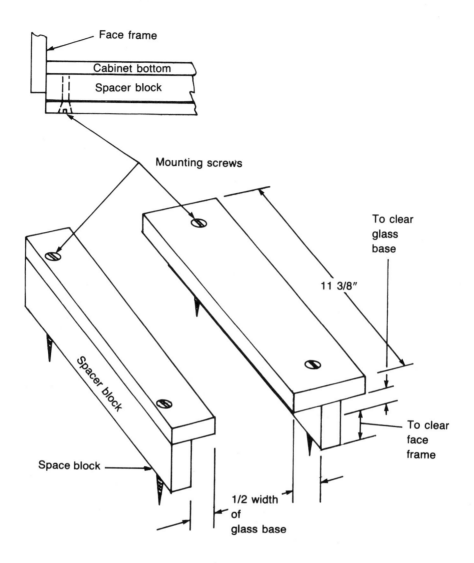

Labels on figure:
Face frame
Cabinet bottom
Spacer block
Mounting screws
To clear glass base
11 3/8"
Spacer block
To clear face frame
Space block
1/2 width of glass base

Fig. 8-11. Glass holder details.

be mounted on any wall cabinet. See Fig. 8-11 for details of construction, which are simple enough. The holders should be constructed and finished prior to mounting on the cabinet. Because the stems and bases of wine glasses may vary from the dimensions given in Fig. 8-12, check the dimensions of your glasses to make sure they fit. The space blocks must, of course, be high enough to allow the glass base to clear the bottom of the face frame. Each assembly should then be mounted to the cabinet bottom with two wood screws.

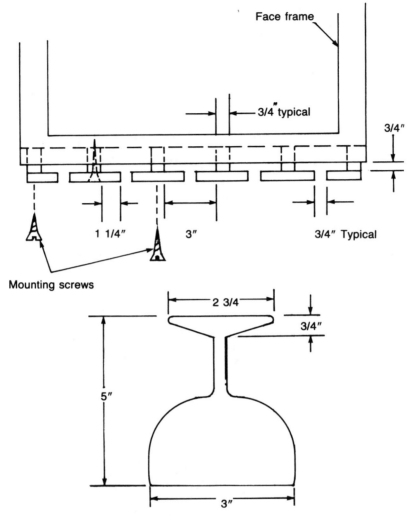

Fig. 8-12. Glass holder dimensions.

Chapter 9

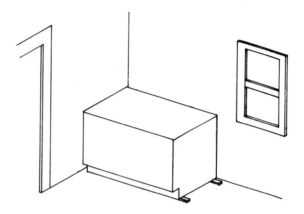

Installing the Cabinet and Top

T HE TYPICAL WALL CABINET WILL SUPPORT A WEIGHT OF about 20 pounds per square foot of shelf area. Obviously, the support of this weight depends principally on correct installation. Proper installation requires the use of screws long enough to reach through the wall cabinet mounting rails and wall board or plaster and into the studs by at least 1″. Usually 3″-by-No.-10 screws will do the trick. Four screws should be the minimum number to hold each cabinet to the studs. In the event that the stud locations do not allow this, toggle bolts may be used as an alternative to the screws.

LEVELING AND SHIMMING

Perhaps the single most important part of installing cabinets is making sure they are level—a subject that was touched on briefly in Chapter 2. First, you must find the "high" spot on the floor. You then measure 34″ vertically from that point and draw a level line along the wall where your cabinet will be located (Fig. 2-2). Base cabinets are normally 34″ high, but if yours are slightly higher or lower, then adjust this measurement accordingly.

With multiple base cabinets, always start at a corner and work outward. This applies whether you are installing a single vanity cabinet or an entire kitchen. Place the cabinet against the wall and, using wedges (thin end over thick end, as shown in Fig. 9-1), place them under each corner until the cabinet is level with the line on the wall. Then carefully lift the cabinet off the wedges and secure the wedges to the floor with a couple of finishing nails or brads.

It is extremely important to make sure that the studs have been located; presumably, you have already marked their locations as discussed in Chapter 2. If not, the wall studs must be found and plainly marked. This can be accomplished in several ways:

• Use a magnetic stud finder found in most hardware stores. This clever device will locate the nails in the walls. If your house has iron water or gas pipes it will also find them.
• After removing the baseboards, you will probably be able to see the nail heads in the dry wall or plaster indicating the studs.
• A finishing nail can be driven into the wall until a stud is found. Tapping the wall and listening for a solid sound will give a clue on the approximate stud location. Of course, drive the nail at a location that will be covered by the cabinets when they are mounted.

Once you have found one stud, the others can be found by measuring, normally 16″. When you think you've located a stud, verify it by driving in a finishing nail. It may be necessary to do this every inch or so until you've located the studs. On wide cabinets, such as 42″, there should be a screw near the center to prevent sagging. As a rule, it would be a good practice to place

Fig. 9-1. Leveling base cabinet with wedges.

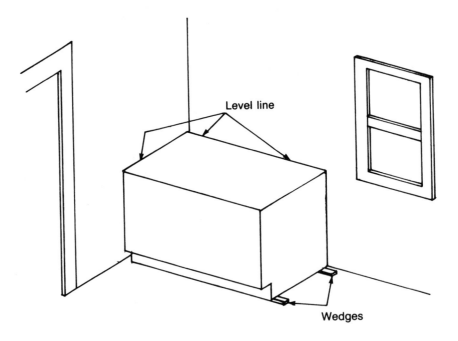

Level line

Wedges

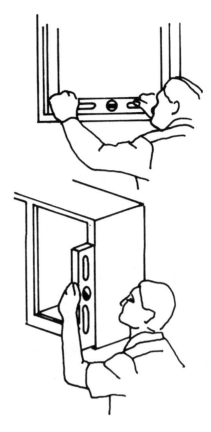

Fig. 9-2. Leveling wall cabinets.

screws not more than 24″ apart.

Measure the distance from the corner (or other reference point) to the stud, and transfer this measurement to the top inside of your cabinet. Drill a pilot hole with an appropriately sized drill. I have found a Screw-Mate invaluable for this (and many other) tasks. It drills a pilot hole, shank clearance hole, and countersinks all at once.

SECURING THE CABINET

A level must be used to accurately install cabinets. Each section should be installed level and plumb. The use of wood shims or wedges between the cabinet back and the wall will accomplish this (see Fig. 9-2). Using your stud markings, drill holes through the wall cabinet mounting rails and mount to the studs with the mounting screws as shown in Fig. 9-3. Do not tighten the mounting screws excessively, because you will cause the wall cabinets to conform to the variations in the wall. If you tighten the mounting screws too much, you will cause racking or twisting in the cabinets. The cabinets are supported by the sheer strength of the fasteners, not the tightness.

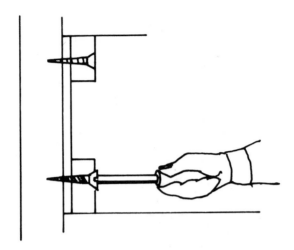

Now you're ready to fasten the base cabinet to the wall. First, recheck to make sure that the cabinet is still level on line, and does not rock or wobble. Check also to make sure there is no space between the back of the cabinet and the wall. If there is, tack two wedges to the studs so that when the cabinet is fastened to the wall it will not be pulled out of plumb. Now screw the cabinet to the wall in at least two places. If it is located in a corner, screw it to each wall. Never nail a cabinet to a wall or floor; always secure it with screws. Cabinets that are nailed to the walls have a tendency to shift. Also, should you or someone else wish to change or replace the cabinets someday, it's likely that they'll be damaged or broken unless screws were used to install them. Cabinets that are properly secured and installed can be easily removed without damage. In fact, I have removed a kitchen cabinet in the middle of a large unit simply by removing the screws that held it to the wall and stiles.

There are a few minor differences between installation of a bathroom vanity and a kitchen cabinet. First, standard dimensions may vary. If your family includes a few "giants," you may want to seriously consider making cabinets that are taller than average. Actually, that's another good reason for building your own. Kitchen cabinets, for example, are generally 24″ deep to accommodate sinks, dishwashers, and the like, whereas vanities are usually 22″ deep. Kitchen wall cabinets, on the other hand, are usually 12″ deep and are mounted 15″ to 18″ above the countertop.

When mounting multiple base cabinets, the procedures are exactly the same as described above: you just have to shim and level for each unit. Once the first unit has been screwed to the wall (the corner is usually secured first), clamp the stiles together (doors removed) with "C" clamps so that the tops and front are flush.

Fig. 9-3. Screwing through mounting rail.

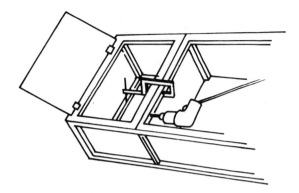

Fig. 9-4. Screwing stiles together.

Using a Screw-Mate or drill and countersink, drill a hole through the stile near the top and bottom of the door hole (Fig. 9-4). Screw the two cabinets together, and then screw the last cabinet to the wall. Repeat this procedure until all base cabinets are secured to the wall (Fig. 9-5).

INSTALLING COUNTERTOPS

With all the base cabinets in place, it's time to install the countertop. If this is your first cabinet attempt, I recommend that your purchase the top premade from the lumberyard. The price should be relatively modest (be sure to shop around) and while the selection may be somewhat limited, buying one will avoid the necessity of learning another skill immediately. Later, I will deal with the subject of making your own countertops. For the moment, let's assume that the top is at hand (if it isn't, skip over this section until you have acquired one, whether prebuilt or homemade).

Mounting countertops is quite easy, actually, although there may be times when you feel like a contortionist. First, remove the drawers and drill into the base cabinet top frame where a stiffener on the countertop crosses it. I have found that hold-down screws

Fig. 9-5. Countersink stile screws.

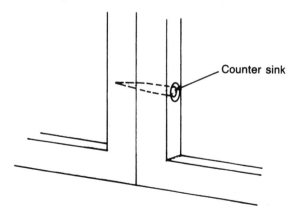

Counter sink

are needed every 2' to 3' in the front and every 3' to 4' in the back. I strongly recommend that you use Phillips head screws (1 1/4" #8 flat head). If you have difficulty finding them, ask your lumberyard (or hardware store) for drywall screws of the same size. Install the screws *up through* the cabinet frame into the countertop.

WALL CABINETS

Usually, there are no wall cabinets used with a vanity. In any event, the installation of a wall cabinet, whether in the bathroom or kitchen, is very similar. When installing wall cabinets, it's important to locate the studs. If the stud locations previously marked for the base cabinets are now obscured, repeat the methods discussed earlier. Make your markings at a level that will be hidden when you hang the wall cabinets; this will save touch-up of plaster or paint after you're through.

If you did not make a set of mini-horses as described in Chapter 4 (Fig. 4-5), you should do so now. The height should be 1/2" less than the distance from the counter to the bottom of the wall cabinet. It's a good idea to predrill mounting holes that match the stud locations. The mounting holes must be drilled in the top structural member. If there is a corner wall cabinet, hang it first and work away from the corner as you did with the base cabinets. Set the mini-horses on the countertop with two scraps of 1/4" plywood placed on top of each one; this will allow easy removal of the mini-horses after the cabinet is fastened to the wall. Place the cabinet to be mounted on the mini-horses, adjust its location (side to side), and screw into the studs through the upper structural member of the cabinet. The process is repeated for each additional wall cabinet to be hung. Be sure that you clamp and screw each set of adjoining stiles together as you proceed.

Sounds simple, doesn't it? Using this mini-horse system, you can install wall cabinets rapidly and accurately every time.

Chapter 10

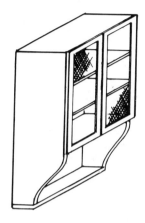

Bathroom Storage

I N PLANNING THEIR BATHROOMS, HOMEOWNERS ALL TOO frequently allow insufficient storage space for the things they use everyday. For example, where do most people store the extra toilet paper or soap for the bathroom? Probably under the sink, in a hall closet, or in the kitchen. In this chapter, I will show you how to create a simple but useful cabinet, one that provides extra storage space in your bathroom while at the same time utilizing space that would otherwise go to waste.

OVER-THE-TANK CABINET

One such space is located above the toilet tank. It's a great place to put a cabinet for extra soap and other toiletries, guest towels, and toilet paper. The cabinet I'm about to describe will allow you to make some mistakes; you can mess up a piece or two without feeling guilty about wasting a lot of material. Because of its modest size, it uses very little material. It also provides an excellent project for the beginner, because its design and construction are relatively easy. At the same time, it includes most of the skills and methods required to make more complicated vanities and kitchen cabinets.

Although the plans and materials list for this cabinet are modest enough to allow complete construction in a weekend, it will take more than a few days to stain and finish it properly. That's because stains and varnishes take so long to dry thoroughly. Once the job is finished, though, I'll predict that your new cabinet will get rave reviews from friends, relatives, and house guests. Perhaps more important, you'll feel a real sense of pride when you realize that you've created and finished a product equal to or better than those in stores. Moreover, its modest cost will encourage you to go back to the shop and tackle another project.

Tools and Materials

Let's first sketch what we have in mind, beginning with the dimensions. It's a good idea to refer back first to Chapter 2 and reread the discourse on sketches and materials lists. You should realize by now that these are important steps in successful cabinetmaking. As shown in Fig. 10-1, our design includes double doors with cane panels, with a shelf below the cabinet. If you prefer, the cane panels can be replaced with raised panels, fabric covered panels, or whatever suits your fancy. The shelf can be omitted if you like, but I feel it adds to the overall look and balance of the cabinet.

The following tools and materials are required:

• Table saw with combination blade (a dado set can also be used, but it is not necessary).

Fig. 10-1. Cabinet for storage above toilet.

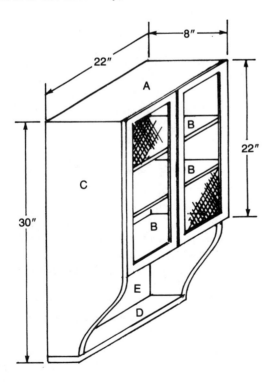

- Saber saw (unless bottom shelf is omitted).
- Glue.
- Sandpaper (if available, use a power sander).
- 3/8" offset semiconcealed, self-closing hinges (two pairs).
- Combination or framing square.
- Tape measure.
- A pair of pipe clamps (helpful but not essential).
- Cane or panel material (about 4 sq.ft.).
- Two pieces of 1"-×-8" pine (#2 common) each 8' long.
- 1/4-pound of 4d finish nails.
- Phillips screwdriver.
- Hammer.
- Stain, varnish, and brushes.
- 600-grit wet or dry sandpaper.
- Six 3/8"-×-1 1/2" dowels.

I can't stress enough the importance of a sketch similar to Fig. 10-1. It provides dimensions and labels so that you can easily create a complete and accurate materials list before you make the journey to the lumberyard. All dimensions shown in Table 10-1 are the final size. That means you should allow a little extra for making final cuts.

Measuring the Doors

Before making up the rest of the materials lists for the face frame and doors, let's sketch out those details too and calculate the size of the doors (which will both be the same). Note the discussion in the previous chapter about leaving space to mount the hinges. That means we can accept a face frame width of 1 3/4". Subtracting 3 1/2" (2 times 1 3/4") from our overall width of 22" leaves a door opening of 18 1/2". The height of the door opening will be the same as the width. Once again, we'll use doors with a lip, so we must now add 1/4" on all sides—leaving 1/8" clearance—to obtain the door's overall width and height. By adding 1/2" (2 times 1/4"), we obtain an overall width (and height) of 19". Because there are two doors, we'll divide by two, leaving a door size of 9 1/2" by 19".

To make things a little easier, let's use the same 1 3/4" wood

Table 10-1. Casework Dimensions.

Label	Qty	Description	Size
T	1	Top	3/4" × 4" × 29 1/4"
B	1	Bottom	3/4" × 4" × 29 1/4"
SL	1	Side, Left	3/4" × 4" × 24"
SR	1	Side, Right	3/4" × 4" × 24"
E	1	Back (plywood)	1/4" × 23 1/4" × 29 1/4"

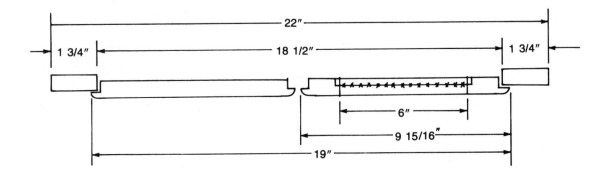

Fig. 10-2. Cabinet cross section dimensions.

for the door rails (horizontal pieces) and stiles (vertical pieces). That will allow us to cut all the stock for the face frame and doors with one saw setting. Figure 10-2 details the cross section of the cabinet face frame and doors, showing the dimensions as outlined above. Figure 10-3 shows the labels for the face frame and doors.

Take time now to summarize your needs before taking off for the lumberyard. You may find that it's helpful to sketch out the needed pieces in a layout similar to that shown in Fig. 10-4, which indicates that two pieces measuring 1"-×-8"-×-10' are required. REMINDER: the lumber dimensions given are those before the board has been dried and planed; thus a 1"-×-8" piece is in actuality about 3/4"-×-7 1/4". Be sure to select boards that are not bowed or cupped, and keep in mind that both boards will be cut; careful selection will therefore allow cutting out most of the knots later on.

The only piece left is the plywood for the back panel. Most lumberyards carry pieces smaller than 4'-×-8', so don't be bashful about asking what they have in stock. If the only small piece of plywood available is 3/8" thick, you can make it fit by cutting the rabbets on the rear of the sides, top, and bottom to a depth of 3/8" instead of 1/4" as shown on the plans.

Cutting the Doors

Using Fig. 10-4 as a guide, lay the pieces out lightly in pencil. Remember to allow enough space between pieces for saw cuts. If knots appear in critical places, such as the ends or where dadoes will fall, adjust the piece accordingly and mark or label each piece before cutting. After both sides of the cabinet (B) have been cut, lay out on one side the curved cut near the bottom, using a compass. (If a compass is not available, use the bottom of a can.) Carefully line up the two sides and clamp them together with a couple of 4d finish nails. That way, when you cut the curved portion, both sides will be identical (see Fig. 10-5).

To prevent mistakes and speed up the cutting process, let's

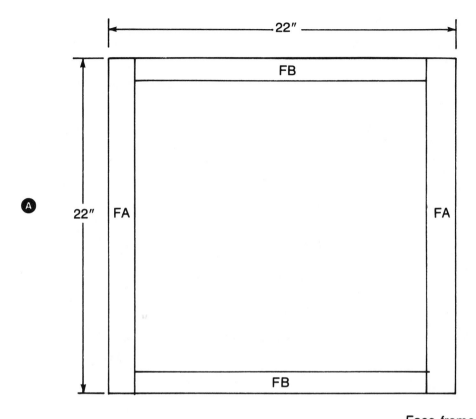

A

22"

22"

FB

FA   FA

FB

Face frame

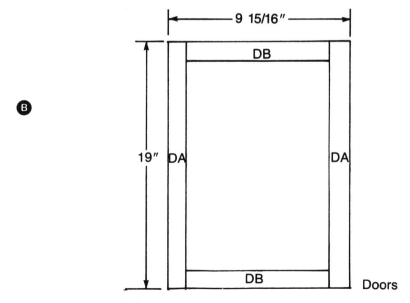

B

9 15/16"

DB

19" DA   DA

DB

Doors

Fig. 10-3. (A) Face frame labels; (B) door labels.

115

← 10' (120") →				
21	21	21	21	30
A	B	B	B	C

FA	DA	FB		DA	
FA	DA	DB	DB	D	C
FB	DA	DB	DB		

make a few more sketches. The sides will initially be the same until they are rabbeted and dadoed; after that they will be mirror images. Figures 10-6 and 10-7 illustrate the cuts made on the left side, the top, and the bottom. When setting up the saw fence to cut the rabbets, check the setting with a piece of scrap; then cut all the rabbets enough to make a suitable recess for the 1/4" plywood back. You will be rabbeting both sides (remember the mirror image) plus the top and bottom. The intermediate shelves are not rabbeted; they are simply cut 1/4" narrower to allow for the back.

Figure 10-8 shows all the pieces cut to size, dadoed, rabbeted,

Fig. 10-4. Piece layout.

Fig. 10-5. Holding two pieces together with finishing nails.

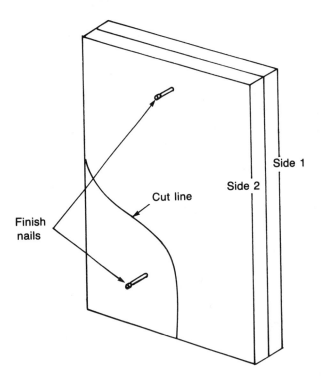

Side 1

Side 2

Cut line

Finish
nails

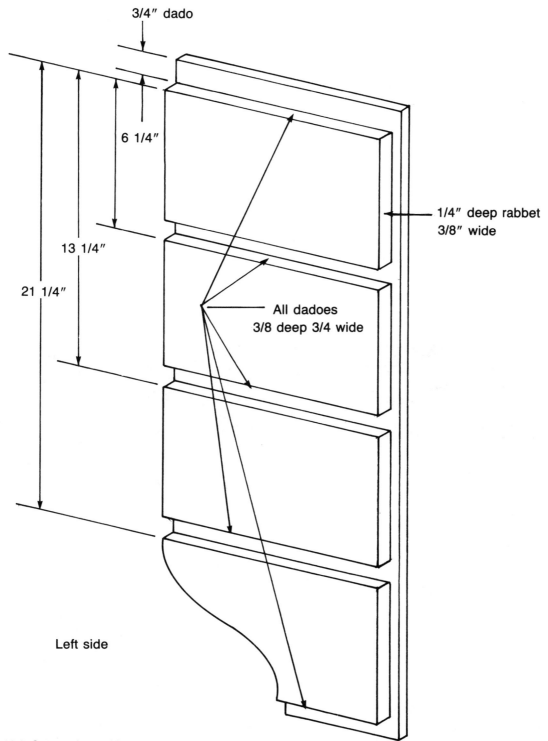

3/4″ dado

6 1/4″

13 1/4″

21 1/4″

1/4″ deep rabbet
3/8″ wide

All dadoes
3/8 deep 3/4 wide

Left side

Fig. 10-6. Cuts made on sides.

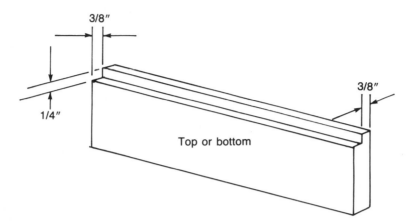

3/8"

1/4"

Top or bottom

3/8"

and ready to put together. Notice that the depth of rabbet and dado are the same: 3/8". This allows you to cut with only one saw depth setting. TIP: when cutting a 3/8" dado or rabbet in 3/4" stock, it is much easier to use a piece of scrap, set the blades or dado set to protrude 3/8" above the saw table, and cut a scrap piece. Next turn the piece over and recut it so the cut is made directly under

Fig. 10-7. Cuts made on top and bottom.

Fig. 10-8. All the pieces needed.

where the first cut was made. Obviously, if the blade is too high, it will cut off the piece completely; but if the blade is too low the piece will still be attached. In this instance, the blade should be raised one half the remaining thickness. Once set, make all the cross grain dadoes or rabbets first, then make the cuts parallel to the grain to minimize splintering. (In general, when clean sharp edges are desired, it's a good idea to place a piece of scrap stock behind the work to prevent splintering.)

Assembly

Now recheck all your cuts. Then prior to applying glue, dry-fit all pieces for a "last chance" check. If everything looks okay, apply glue and clamp the work together as shown in Fig. 10-9. Notice that the work is clamped so that the back can be installed. The back must be installed while the glue on the casework is still wet, otherwise the case may not be square. Install the back with brads and glue, loosening the clamps when necessary to allow for straightening. When applying the glue for the back, be careful not to use an excessive amount and keep the glue away from the inside edges. Too much glue will squeeze out onto the inside of the cabinet, mak-

Fig. 10-9. Clamped work assembly.

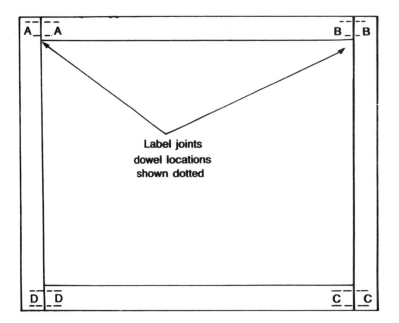

Label joints
dowel locations
shown dotted

Fig. 10-10. Face frame layout.

ing removal very difficult. Glue that is not removed will prevent stain from entering the wood, causing an unsightly clear spot.

While the casework glue is drying, it's time to begin work on the face frame, cutting all the pieces to their length and laying them out as shown in Fig. 10-10. It is important to label each frame piece carefully. If you haven't already done so, mark them with letters as shown. This extra marking may seem superfluous, but it isn't. It's too easy to mix up the pieces and, as a result, drill the wrong end or side. Better to be safe than sorry; besides, it makes dry-fitting a snap. Before gluing up the face frame, lay the dry-fitted assembly on top of the casework (which surely is dry now) to make certain it's the right size. When the face frame is glued, place it on the front of the casework and tack it on with a couple of 4d finish nails. This will ensure that the frame isn't racked and is square to the cabinet; as a result, when you glue them together later, they will match each other. Next, cut the rails (horizontal pieces) to their exact size, leaving the stiles (vertical pieces) long so they can be trimmed after the glue has dried.

Figure 10-11 shows all the door parts, except for the cane and the splines that support the cane. If you'd rather not use cane, decorative pierced aluminum is available in many stores. It too will make a handsome door panel and is held in place the same way as the cane. In studying Fig. 10-11, did you notice the dotted lines? They represent the dado, which is deeper at the ends to allow for the tenons on the ends of the rails (shown in the end view). This type of dado is cut in two operations: first, a dado 1/4″ wide and

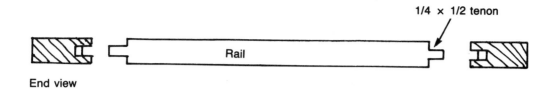

1/4 × 1/2 tenon

End view

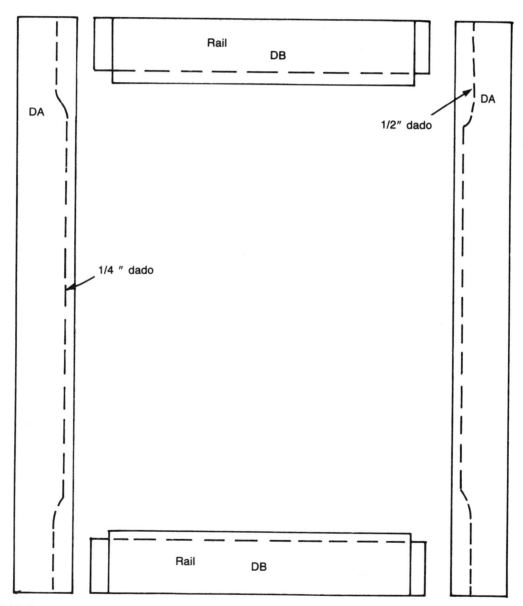

Rail

DB

DA

1/2" dado

DA

1/4 " dado

Rail

DB

Fig. 10-11. Door parts.

1/4″ deep on the inside surface of both rails and stiles; and second, a second dado with the cutters raised to cut 1/2″ deep at both ends of the stiles. Using scrap stock of the same thickness as the stiles and rails, carefully set the ripping fence so that the dado will cut exactly in the center. This means that either face of the stile can be against the saw's fence, and the dado cut will be in the same place. Clamp a piece of scrap to the rip fence to act as a stop so that each stile dado is the same depth (1/4″-×-1/2″). If you prefer, dowels can be used to hold the rails and stiles together. If you choose this method, drill for the dowels before cutting the 1/4″-×-1/4″ dado for the panel.

Assuming you don't have a router, we can use an alternate method for removing the back side of the dado, which is necessary to allow for the cane panel installation. Reset the rip fence so that the left side of the blade is 1/4″ from the fence. Clamp scrap blocks to the fence as shown in Fig. 10-12. This will limit the travel of the rail and allow you to cut the center section. When making such cuts, which must be started "blind," think through what you'll be

Fig. 10-12. Stop blocks on rip fence.

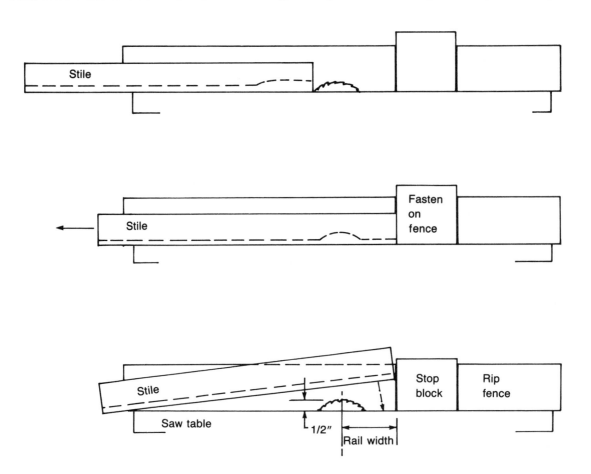

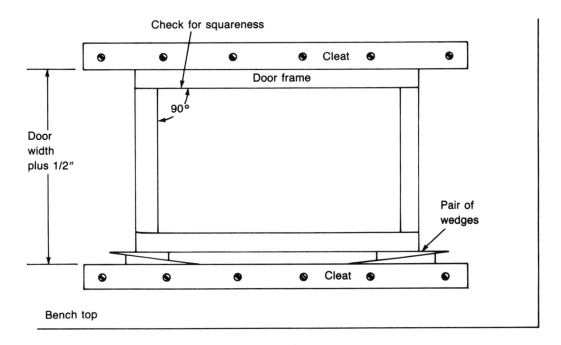

Check for squareness

Cleat

Door frame

90°

Door
width
plus 1/2"

Pair of
wedges

Cleat

Bench top

Fig. 10-13. Clamping with cleats on bench.

doing. Carelessness here could result in a damaged stile, injury, or both. With the rear end of the stile resting against the block, and its edge against the fence, carefully lower the front end of the stile to the saw table. The saw blade will by now have cut a blind slot; this will lengthen as the stile is pushed forward until the forward stop is reached. Do not lift the pieces up while the saw is running. Turn off the saw, and after it stops, remove the stile.

Repeat this operation for the other three stiles. Then, with all four stiles complete, remove the stop blocks and rip off the dado on the side of each rail. The scrap stock—if it survives—can be used for the splines. If it was broken in the process, however, cut new pieces.

The next step is to dry-fit your door parts and glue them together. When clamping doors, it is important to remember the following points: make sure the frames are square if necessary—place a scrap piece of plywood where the cane will go for the time being; and make sure the frame is flat—a warped door is all but impossible to remedy. After you're sure everything has been done properly, glue the pieces together using pipe clamps. If you have no pipe clamps, Fig. 10-13 shows how a benchtop with temporary cleats nailed (or screwed) to it can be used to clamp the door frame while the glue dries. The secret here is the four wedges we learned about in Chapter 4 (and don't forget the jig to make them).

While the glue is drying on the doors, the face frame can be glued to the casework. Recheck to make sure that the fit is correct. Tack 4d finish nails somewhere near two diagonally opposite

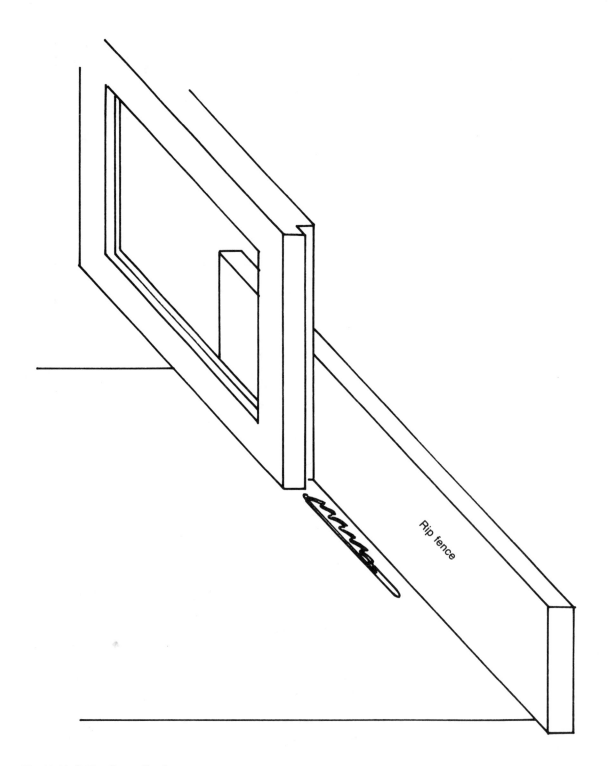

Rip fence

Fig. 10-14. Cutting lips on the doors.

corners. Remove the frame, but do not remove the finish nails; they will enable you to locate the face frame on the case without it sliding out of place. Apply glue to the rear side of the face frame and the edges of the casework where the face frame will rest. Wet all the surfaces, but don't be overly generous with the glue. Attach the face frame to the casework and hammer home the two "locating" finish nails. Drive additional 4d nails through the frame every 8" to 10".

Now that we're nearly finished with the woodworking aspects of this project, the only thing left is to rabbet all the edges of the doors to provide a lip. The normal rabbet is 3/8" by 3/8", so set the saw fence to cut 3/8" from the left of the saw blade and set the blade height for 3/8". First make all the cuts with the door on the edges (as shown in Fig. 10-14). Remember, the rabbet will be cut on the rear side of the door, the same side on which the panel is mounted. Finally, with the door laying flat on the saw table, make the second cut, at the ends first, then on the sides. Do not stand directly to the rear of the blade, because those "darts" can be propelled rearward at high speed.

Except for finish sanding, there remains only the cane panels to install, and that should be done last. The time you spend sanding will determine what quality finish you end up with, so take your time. Refer to Chapter 6 on finishing.

Installing the Cane Panels

The first step is to cut the cane panels about 1" wider and longer than the rabbeted opening on the back of the doors. Center the cane in the opening and staple the middle of a long side. Next pull the caning over tight to the other long side and place another staple in the middle. NOTE: an ordinary household stapler will work fine.

Repeat this process, first stapling the middle of one end and then the other. Try not to pull the caning out of shape. Systematically pull each corner out tight and staple it in place, then check the front of the door. Does it look right? If you're satisfied, apply enough glue to the splines so that some of it will pass through the cane to the rabbet cuts in the stiles and rails. Next, nail the splines in place and set aside for 24 hours while the glue dries.

When the glue which holds the cane panels in place has dried, dampen the cane on both sides with water and sponge. This will tighten the cane. When the finish is applied—assuming it's polyurethane—be sure to apply it to both sides of the cane.

The doors can be hinged in the same manner as previously discussed in Chapter 7. Hanging the cabinet can best be done with screw eyes and heavy-duty picture hangers; or you can install screws through the back into the wall studs. Figure 10-15 shows the finished result.

Fig. 10-15. Finished cabinet.

MEDICINE CABINET

Another common storage space is the medicine cabinet. Although the construction of a medicine cabinet is similar to the above-tank cabinet, there are significant differences, the most important of which is the fact that a mirror on the door is a must. There are two ways to provide the mirrored front: instead of making two doors, make one and use a mirror instead of the cane panel described in the previous cabinet; use commercial tracks and provide two mirrors that slide in the tracks, in a manner similar to sliding closet doors. Because the construction for the sliding doors is somewhat different, I will cover its construction.

This cabinet will also allow you to make some mistakes by messing up a piece or two without wasting a lot of material, because it, too, uses very little material and its design and construction are relatively easy. It also includes most of the skills and methods required to make more complicated cabinets.

By now you know a sketch of what we have in mind with dimensions is essential. This cabinet, as shown in Fig. 10-16, does not have wooden shelves, nor will they be fixed the way they were in the cabinet designed to hang over the toilet. Instead, we will provide slots in the sides in which glass shelves will go. Notice, also, that in this instance we do not use a face frame, partly because it will reduce the size of the mirrored front, and also because it would

Fig. 10-16. Dimensions and labels of medicine cabinet.

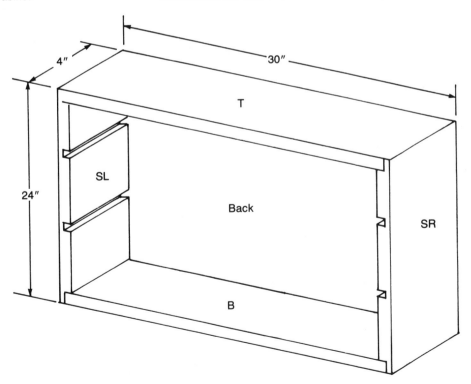

127

not allow you to change where you'd like the shelves placed.

Except for the mirrors and glass shelves, the tools and materials required are really the same as those previously required, so there's no need to relist them. The mirrors and shelves should be double weight and have ground edges. A local store selling mirrors and glass will fill your needs at a modest price.

Figure 10-16 provides dimensions and labels so that you can easily create a complete and accurate materials list before you make the journey to the lumberyard. Allow a little extra material for making final cuts because the dimensions shown in Fig. 10-16 are the final size.

A few more sketches so we don't miscut the dadoes will be helpful. The sides initially will be the same until they are rabbeted and dadoed; after that they will be mirror images. Figures 10-17 and 10-18 illustrate the cuts made on the left side, the top, and the

Fig. 10-17. Cuts made on sides.

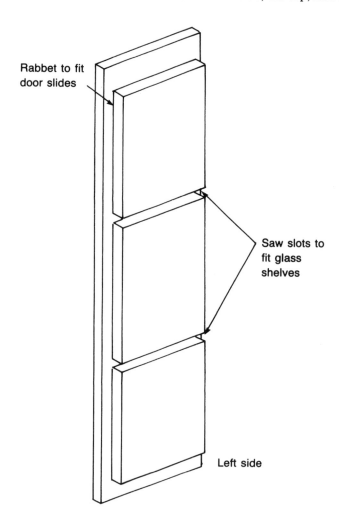

Rabbet to fit door slides

Saw slots to fit glass shelves

Left side

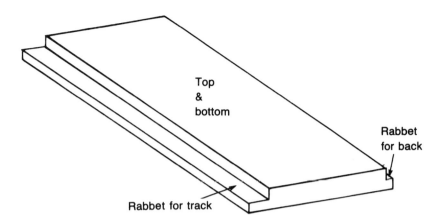

Top
&
bottom

Rabbet
for back

Rabbet for track

Fig. 10-18. Cuts made on top and bottom.

bottom. When setting up the saw fence to cut the rabbets, check the setting with a piece of scrap; then cut all the rabbets enough to make a suitable recess for the 1/4″ plywood back. You will be rabbeting both sides (remember the mirror image) plus the top and bottom.

Recheck all your cuts, dry-fit all pieces, and if everything looks OK, apply glue and clamp the work together. Remember to clamp the work so that the back can be installed while the glue on the casework is still wet, otherwise the case may not be square. Install the back with brads and glue, loosening the clamps when necessary to allow for straightening. When applying the glue for the back, be careful not to use an excessive amount and keep the glue away from the inside edges. Too much glue will squeeze out onto the inside of the cabinet and removing it will be very difficult.

Hanging the cabinet can be accomplished with screws through the back into the wall studs.

Chapter 11

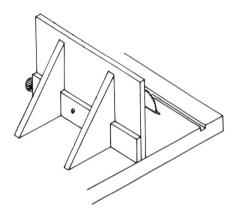

Odds and Ends

O VER THE YEARS, YOU WILL COME ACROSS USEFUL BITS OF information that will make your cabinetry and woodworking skills more professional and easier. These bits of knowledge don't exactly fit in every project, so I've added them here as a sort of general reference section.

SAFETY COMES FIRST

Safety is a topic that frequently is ignored in many do-it-yourself books, perhaps because the authors are afraid the subject will scare off beginners. Well, it certainly shouldn't scare off anyone who is sincerely interested in maintaining his or her health. Most of us start out life with two eyes, two hands, and ten fingers, and I know we'd all like to end up that way! So here are a few common sense safety rules for all woodworkers to observe.

- If you are tired, either physically or mentally, stick to those minor tasks that do not involve the use of power tools.
- When using power tools, think out the operation *thoroughly* before you begin to cut. If you run into a snag, shut off the power and replan. Remember, many power tools are capable of seriously injuring you.
- NEVER assume the guards on your power saw are foolproof

preventers of accidents. (Author's note: When I was 12, my father gave me my 8″ table saw. He told me that it did not have a guard because he wanted me to see the blade as a constant reminder that it was capable of cutting off my fingers. I have never forgotten that—and I have never injured myself on the table saw.)

• Whenever possible, use pusher sticks (Fig. 11-1) to keep your hands and fingers as far away from cutting edges as possible.

• Do not stand directly behind the line of a circular saw blade; knots or small pieces of wood that become pinched between the blade and fence can fly backward like missiles.

• Expose only that portion of the saw blade required to cut through the wood's thickness. One exception: hollow ground blades should be fully exposed.

• I strongly recommend wearing a safety mask or goggles. Not only do they protect your eyes from flying debris, but should something fly into your eyes, you may jerk your hands away involuntarily and cause an injury.

• Make sure that your shop and workbench have proper lighting; it's as important as having the right kind of tools. In my shop, which measures about 12′- × -24′; I have six dual-lamp 48″ fluorescent fixtures. You may not need that many. Just remember, though, that poor lighting is not only a safety hazard, it's a major cause of poor workmanship.

• A roll-up power cord above the work table is another good safety device. It removes the danger of tripping over wires and extension cords. Also, it's a good idea to place your work table in the middle of the shop floor so that you can walk and work on all four sides.

HARDWARE

When shopping for cabinet hardware, either locally or by mail, you will be confronted by many styles and kinds of cabinet latches, hinges, and door edges. Several years ago, I abandoned the use of a magnet catch in favor of the self-closing hinge. It costs more

Fig. 11-1. Pusher stick.

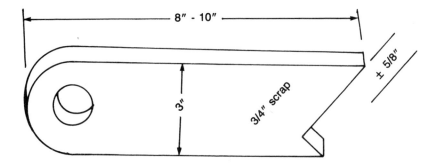

than a regular hinge, but less than the hinge and catch. During the design stages, you made a decision on whether the doors would be flush or half-lap (there is also an inset, which is not recommended for beginners). If you chose half-lap (Fig. 11-2), then you will need the 3/8″ offset when selecting the hinges.

RAISED PANELS AND MOLDINGS

Doors for the cabinet can also have raised panels, but this requires more tools and more fixtures, such as the *panel raising fence* shown in Fig. 11-3. To make good raised panels, a belt sander is needed. When I make raised panels, I set the saw at approximately 10° to the table. Then the panel blank is run through the saw with the ripping gauge set so that the blade barely comes through the surface (Fig. 11-4). I rip each edge in turn, then return the blade to 90°. Using a rip-gauge, I then reset to intersect the previous cuts (Fig. 11-5). Remember to reset the blade protrusion so that it just cuts off the scrap piece. The thin edge of the finished door must be slightly less than 1/4″; otherwise, it won't fit in the dado of the door frame (Fig. 11-6).

In Chapter 5, applied molding was discussed (see Fig. 5-4). The

Fig. 11-2. Typical hardware.

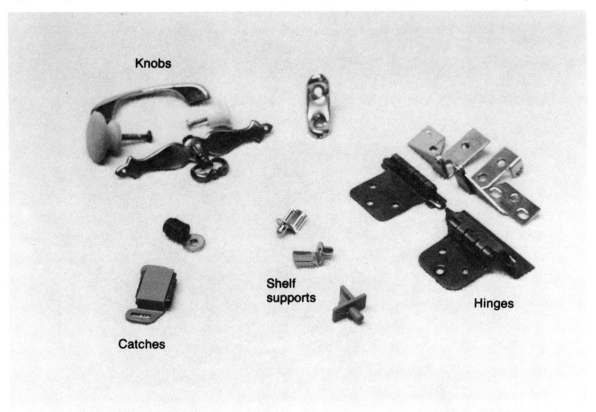

Knobs

Shelf
supports

Hinges

Catches

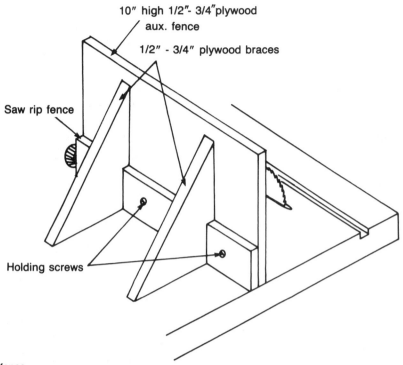

Fig. 11-3. Panel raising fence.

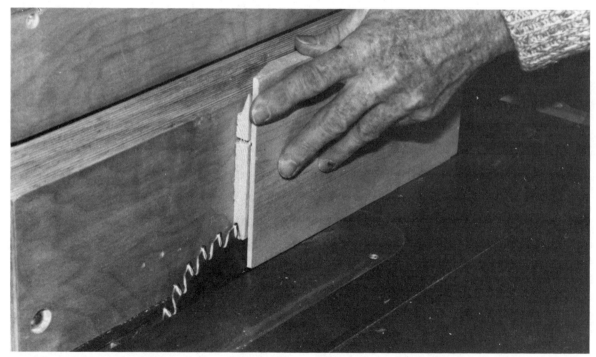

Fig. 11-4. Raised panel angle cut.

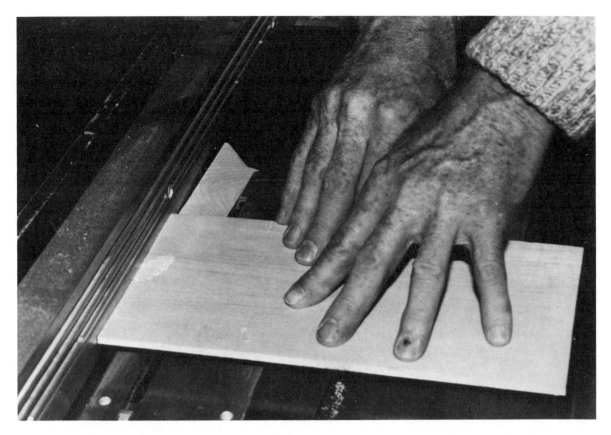

Fig. 11-5. Raised panel face cut.

molding corner joints must be mitered; this can be done by hand or with the miter-cutting fixture shown in Fig. 11-7. This fixture is also very handy for cutting all kinds of moldings for picture frames.

INSTALLING SINKS

Sinks or basins are either self-rimming, or they mount with the aid of a special frame. All sinks have a hole layout printed on the carton; simply follow the directions that come with the sink. To cut holes in the finished countertop, you'll need a carbide blade in a saber (jig) saw, but first drill a hole to make it easier to start. If you are purchasing the countertop, by all means pay the few dollars extra for having the cut out done for you.

HINT: If you know where the sink will be placed, and you will be doing the application of the laminate, precut the hole in the substrate first. It will be much less work.

SOFFITS

When wall cabinets are hung, they often hang below a *soffit*. A soffit is false work built to close in the space between the tops of cabinets and the ceiling. Depending on individual taste and kitchen decor, you may or may not want to build a soffit above your cabinets. Some will want to use soffits to avoid the tops of cabinets becoming dust catchers. Others will want to retain the space above their cabinets to place objects such as beer mugs, baskets, antique kitchen implements, or infrequently used kitchen objects.

Building soffits is relatively easy, particularly if plywood paneling suits your taste. If you prefer drywall or sheetrock soffits, then a bit more work will be necessary to tape over joints and cover the nails.

Hanging sheetrock is a skill that is not in the preview of this book. The key word is *patience*.

Hanging a wood soffit requires only that you know where the ceiling joists and studs are located, so that you can fasten the soffits to them. The process of locating studs was discussed earlier in Chapter 2, so you should already know how to do this. Ceiling joists are located in the same manner. If the ceiling joists run parallel to the wall on which the cabinets will be hung, the wall studs alone will support the soffit. Figure 11-8 shows one way to make

Fig. 11-6. Finished raised panel.

Fig. 11-7. Miter cutting fixture.

a soffit using strapping, pine scraps, and plywood. Use wood screws or ring nails to hold it all together. Although this method is unconventional, it certainly will do the job. The soffit, of course must be longer and wider than the wall cabinets themselves to allow for trim molding. Calculate the height from known dimensions.

For example, if your ceiling is 8' (96") from the floor, and the counter is 36" high, with the 30" high wall cabinets set 16" above the counter, you will need a soffit that is 14" high (96 − 36 − 16 − 30 = 14). Do not cover the soffit frame; in fact, do not put strapping on the front in the belief that this will make it easier to screw the soffit to the studs. Instead, use a few pieces of strapping and some "C" clamps to hold the soffit frame up as it is secured to the wall. Why not use nails? Because there is less chance for a costly slip-up with screws; should you make a mistake, it's much easier to remove screws than nails. Make sure though, that the wood screws are long enough to penetrate the studs at least 3/4".

HINT: Phillips head screws are far easier to handle when doing awkward jobs like this.

LIGHTING

An important part of a well designed, functional kitchen is the lighting. Do not pass this off as a job that can be done later. If additional wiring or switches are required, the time for making these changes is before you install new cabinets, not after. In fact, the lighting plan should be considered before you even begin to build the cabinets. Suppose you plan on under-cabinet lighting: you'll want to make the lower edge of the face frame wide enough to hide the fixture from view. That takes careful planning before the first piece of wood is cut.

Basically, there are three general types of lighting used in kitchens: track lights; ceiling fixtures; and under-cabinet fixtures. A proper lighting scheme should provide at least enough illumination to observe the work and tools at hand without strain. After all, knives and sharp utensils are used in a kitchen, so good lighting is important to prevent accidents. Light placement should be carefully thought out too. It should avoid casting shadows on the working surfaces in the kitchen area, and it should not be blinding.

The least expensive and perhaps the least effective lighting is done with ceiling fixtures. Some excellent ones are available, however, so it may be well worth a trip to the local hardware or lighting fixture store to review the various models available and their costs. In doing so, keep in mind the possibility of lowering the ceiling far enough to install a *suspended ceiling* (with the lighting above). Another alternative is to use *recessed fixtures* in the ceiling. When properly placed, this method can provide excellent lighting at moderate cost.

Fig. 11-8. Soffit construction.

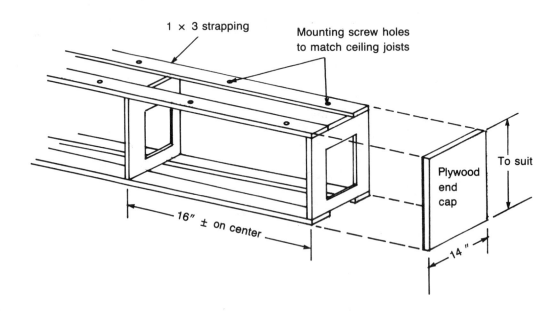

Unless you do your own wiring, the expense of having an electrician do the wiring may offset the lower costs. Also, because holes must be cut in the ceiling to mount the recessed lights, careful planning is important. Mistakes made here will be difficult to coverup. If you plan to put in soffits, by the way, why not extend them in front of the wall cabinets, enough to mount your recessed fixtures behind them? Review the section on making soffits and make them about 12″ deeper than shown. Plan ahead, so that intermediate braces on the soffit do not fall where you plan to locate a fixture. In fact, a fixture hole can be cut in a soffit more easily before it is mounted.

Track lighting is somewhat expensive but quite versatile. Should the fixtures appear to be placed improperly, track lights can be easily moved. Also, if the lighting scheme proves insufficient, another fixture is easy to add. My kitchen is in a post and beam house, in which post-construction wiring is extremely difficult. My solution was to use track lights, with the tracks mounted on the side of the ceiling beams. Coupled with the track lights, I have used a soffit/valance light over the sink and flourescent fixtures under the cabinets. This combination offers the best of both worlds.

RESOURCES

The most likely place to look for lumber is in a lumberyard, but don't overlook other sources. Some of my cabinets were made from wood salvaged from table leaves. Used furniture from a flea market or auction can provide extremely high quality lumber at a modest cost, but don't forget to allow for your investment in time spent disassembling and removing the finish.

If you live in or near an urban area, check out the local house wreckers and salvage yards. They are frequently in the business of tearing down old mansions that are loaded with walnut and cherry paneling. An inquiry could result in a treasure trove of well seasoned hardwood. As a practical matter, the older the wood you find, the greater its quality is apt to be.

In rural areas, you may locate a sawmill close by that can supply you with green, air-dried, or sometimes kiln-dried wood at considerable savings. Look in the Yellow Pages (under sawmills), and you may be pleasantly surprised.

Following is a listing of various mail order sources I have used with good results:

Albert Constantine and Son, Inc.
2050 East Chester Road
Bronx, NY 10461
1-800-223-8087

Hardwoods, veneers, wood inlay kits, specialty hand tools, cane/caning materials, upholstery tools and materials, hardware, finishing materials, adhesives, moldings, how-to books, inlays, marquetry supplies, clock parts, power tools.

Silvo Hardware Co.
2205 Richmond Street
Philadelphia, PA 19125
(215) 423-6200

Nationally advertised brands of tools: Stanley, Coastal, Rockwell, Milwaukee, Skil, Wen, Wellsaw, Dremel, Foredom, Millers Falls, Lufkin, Irwin, Dasco, Remington, Jorgenson, Vermont American, Disston, Oldham, Nicholson, Plumb, X-acto, Estwing, Marshalltown, Hanson, Ridgid, Greenlee, Marples, Record, Knape and Vogt, Black & Decker, Makita, Bosch, General, Channel Lock, Toolkraft. An extremely wide range of hand and power tools at very reasonable prices.

J. Cheaps & Sons
Cheaps Pond Park, Box 7199
Warrensville, OH 44128
1-800-821-4142

Some unusual and hard to find tools here, costs low on some items. Variety limited.

Woodcraft
313 Montvale Avenue
Woburn, MA 01801

Imported and domestic tools and accessories, and woodworking books.

Minnesota Woodworkers Supply Co.
Rogers, MN 55374

Veneers, inlays, picture framing, furniture trim, stains, books and craft plans, caning supplies, finishing materials.

Craftsman Wood Service Company
2729 S. Mary Street
Chicago, IL 60608

Choice dimension sizes and sheet plywoods both domestic and imported, hand and power tools, inlay bandings and moldings, turned legs, upholstery and lamp supplies, cabinet hardware, etc.

Maurice L. Condon Co., Inc.
248 Ferris Avenue
While Plains, NY 10603
(914) 946-4111

Domestic and foreign hardwoods, including most sizes from 1″ to 4″ in thickness. Ash, basswood, birch, butternut, cherry, chestnut, ebony, maple, oak, poplar, rosewood, teak, walnut. Softwoods include sugar pine, cypress, cedar, spruce, and others.

Educational Lumber Company, Inc.
P.O. Box 5373
Asheville, NC 28803

Specializes in Appalachian hardwoods. Kiln-dried, cabinet-grade wood plus a guarantee for every board foot. Veneers and turnings.

Brookstone
Vose Farm Road
Peterborough, NH 03458

Large variety of tools; many unusual or hard to find.

Industrial Abrasives Co.
P.O. Box 1252
Reading, PA 19603

Sanding belts at exceptionally low prices.

MAGAZINES

Fine Woodworking
The Taunton Press, Inc.
52 Church Hill Road
Newtown, CT 06470

Workbench
P.O. Box 5966
Kansas City, MO 64111

Better Homes & Gardens
Locust at 17th
Des Moines, IA 50380-0625

Handyman
P.O. Box N-1980
Marion, OH 43306

Index

Index

Other Bestsellers From TAB

☐ **66 FAMILY HANDYMAN® WOOD PROJECTS**

Here are 66 practical, imaginative, and decorative projects . . . literally something for every home and every woodworking skill level from novice to advanced cabinetmaker: room dividers, a free-standing corner bench, china/book cabinet, coffee table, desk and storage units, a built-in sewing center, even your own Shaker furniture reproductions! 210 pp., 306 illus. 7″ × 10″.

Paper $14.95   **Hard $21.95**
Book No. 2632

☐ **BUILDING OUTDOOR PLAYTHINGS FOR KIDS, with Project Plans—Barnes**

Imagine the delight of your youngsters—children or grandchildren—when you build them their own special backyard play area complete with swings, climbing bars, sandboxes, even an A-frame playhouse their own size or a treehouse where they can indulge in their own imaginary adventures. Best of all, discover how you can make exciting, custom-designed play equipment at a fraction of the cost of ordinary, ready-made swing sets or sandbox units! It's all here in this practical, step-by-step guide to planning and building safe, sturdy outdoor play equipment. 240 pp., 213 illus., 7″ × 10″.

Paper $12.95   **Hard $21.95**
Book No. 1971

☐ **HARDWOOD FLOORS—INSTALLING, MAINTAINING AND REPAIRING—Ramsey**

Do-it-yourself expert Dan Ramsey gives you all the guidance you need to install, restore, maintain, or repair all types of hardwood flooring at costs far below those charged vices. From details on how to select the type of wood floors best suited to your home, to time- and money-saving ways to keep your floors in tip-top condition . . . nothing has been left out. 160 pp., 230 illus. 4 pages in full color. 7″ × 10″.

Paper $10.95   **Hard $18.95**
Book No. 1928

☐ **PANELING WITH SOLID LUMBER, including projects—Ramsey**

Home remodeling expert Dan Ramsey shows you how to use solid wood paneling to give almost any room in your home a new look that's comfortable, convenient, economical, and practically maintenance-free plus gives you an exciting selection of projects. Included are step-by-step directions for building a cedar closet . . . storm doors and shutters . . . a bathroom partition . . . a sauna decor for your bath . . . storage walls . . . a home bar . . . an attic study . . . book cabinet . . . and more! 192 pp., 288 illus. 7″ × 10″.

Paper $12.95   **Hard $18.95**
Book No. 1868

☐ **TILE FLOORS—INSTALLING, MAINTAINING AND REPAIRING—Ramsey**

Now you can easily install resilient or traditional hard tiles on both walls and floors. Find out how to buy quality resilient floor products at reasonable cost . . . and discover the types and sizes of hard tiles available. Get step-by-step instructions for laying out the floor, selecting needed tools and adhesives, cutting tiles, applying adhesives, and more. 192 pp., 200 illus. 4 pages in full color. 7″ × 10″.

Paper $12.95   **Book No. 1998**

☐ **THE COMPUTER FURNITURE PLAN AND PROJECT BOOK—Wiley**

Now, with the help of this first-of-its-kind handbook, even a novice can build good looking, functional, and low-cost computer furniture that's custom-designed for your own special needs—tables, stands, desks, modular or built-in units, even a posture supporting kneeling chair! Computer hobbyist and craftsman Jack Wiley provides all the step-by-step guidance, detailed project plans, show-how illustrations, and practical customizing advice . . . even basic information on tools, materials, and construction techniques. 288 pp., 385 illus. 7″ × 10″.

Paper $15.95   **Hard $23.95**
Book No. 1949

☐ **DO-IT-YOURSELF DESIGNER WINDOWS**

If the cost of custom-made draperies puts you in a state of shock . . . if you've had trouble finding window coverings of any kind for cathedral or other problem windows . . . or if you're unsure of what type of window decor would look right in your home . . . here's all the advice and information you've been searching for. It's a complete, hands-on guide to selecting, measuring, making, and installing just about any type of window treatment imaginable.

You'll even get an expert's insight into selection and installation of decorative storm windows and thermal windows, stained glass windows, woven or wooden blinds, and workable treatments for problem areas. 272 pp., 414 illus. Large Format (7″ × 10″).

Paper $14.95   **Hard $21.95**
Book No. 1922

☐ **58 HOME SHELVING AND STORAGE PROJECTS—Blandford**

From a two-shelf book rack or table-top organizer to a paneled chest, basic room divider, or hall locker . . . from shelves or a spoon rack to a period reproduction of a Shaker cabinet or a Welsh dresser, you'll be amazed at the variety fo projects included. And, each one includes easy-to-follow, step-by-step directions, plenty of show-how drawings, and complete materials list. 288 pp., 27 illus. 7″ × 10″.

Paper $14.95   **Book No. 1844**

Other Bestsellers From TAB

About the Author

WILLIAM P. GODLEY HAS BEEN BUILDING THINGS WITH wood since he was an 8-year-old growing up in Montclair, New Jersey. He acquired his first power tool (an 8″ table saw) when he was 12, and since then, he has accumulated an impressive array of power and hand tools.

In 1952, Bill Godley designed his own home in El Paso, Texas, and he has been at it every since, building, restoring, and designing homes. One was an eighteenth century colonial farmhouse in Bucks County, Pennsylvania; another was a 35-foot dormer added to a house in Hatboro, Pennsylvania; and still another was a two-story colonial home in Maple Glen, Pennsylvania. He has also built garages, horse barns, and more than 50 pieces of fine custom furniture, including window seats (18th century replicas), a cherry Governor Winthrop desk, cobblers' benches, a 7′ by 12′ cherry breakfront, trestle tables, and candlestick tables. He has worked extensively on kitchens, as this book attests, including custom cabinetry and countertops.

Godley's business career began in 1951, (shortly after five years of engineering and liberal arts at Bucknell University), with Douglas Aircraft, where he worked on missile design. Later he transferred to White Sands Proving Ground, where he was in charge of NIKE missile modification for flight testing. In 1955, he worked for C.V. Construction Co., in El Paso, as superintendent of field construction. In 11 months, 55 houses were built under his supervision. He began a long and successful career in 1956 with the Honeywell organization in the Philadelphia area, serving as supervisor of design drafting and engineering records; manager of manufacturing engineering, tool design, photo lab, and process engineering; and manager of engineering models and service.

In 1973, Godley became general manager of radio station WPRJ in Parsippany-Troy Hills, New Jersey, which he and his brother built, staffed, and equipped. He started his own business of building and custom remodeling in Newtown, Connecticut, in 1977. He now lives in Cotuit, Massachusetts, on Cape Cod, where he recently completed his own energy-efficient home. He is an avid sailor and owner of a 26-foot sloop, so when he has time from his Construction Consulting business and U.S. Coast Guard Auxiliary duties as Public Education officer, that's where you'll find him.

Bill Godley also points with pride to his 35-year romance with amateur theater as a set designer and builder. His elaborate and highly acclaimed sets include a full-scale, 60-foot cross section of a railway coach capable of carrying 12 "passengers" (for "Music Man"); a two-story living room set for "My Fair Lady" featuring a practical balcony that could be moved from the stage in less than 30 seconds; and a self-supporting spiral staircase built on rollers for the musical "Mame."